THE EXTREMI

GADFLIES OF AMER
SOCIETY

Jules Archer
History for Young Readers

THE EXTREMISTS

GADFLIES OF AMERICAN SOCIETY

JULES ARCHER

Foreword by Kathleen Krull

Sky Pony Press
NEW YORK

Historical texts often reflect the time period in which they were written, and new information is constantly being discovered. This book was originally published in 1964, and much has changed since then. While every effort has been made to bring this book up to date, it is important to consult multiple sources when doing research.

To
Edith Margolis Keyshore, without whom not only this book but fourteen others and over a thousand magazine pieces as well might never have appeared

CONTENTS

FOREWORD   ix

1. What Is Extremism?   1
2. Ear-Slicers, Witch-Hunters, and Roughnecks   13
3. The Extremists of 1776   25
4. "March with Me into the Towns!"   36
5. Mob Hysteria Against Masons and Catholics   48
6. Attacks on Privilege   61
7. The Extremist World of Horace Greeley   73
8. Imperialists, Vigilantes, and Know-Nothings   85
9. Civil War Extremists, the K.K.K., and Indian-Killers   97
10. Monopolists, Bomb-Throwers, and Saloon-Wreckers   110
11. "By George and By Jingo!"   121
12. Robber Barons, Wobblies, and Super-Patriots   133
13. Jazz Age and Depression Extremists   146
14. Hitlerites and Stalinites   158
15. McCarthyism Falls; Birchism Rises   170
16. Extremism in the Sixties   182

BIBLIOGRAPHY   199

INDEX   202

ABOUT THE AUTHOR   211

FOREWORD

by Kathleen Krull

Forty-six years ago, noted author Jules Archer published this book, *The Extremists*. What was he trying to do? Nothing less than to tell the whole history of the United States. But, with characteristic cleverness, he uses a catchy and intriguing word—extremist—as a lens.

Archer defines *extremists* broadly: "Those in American history who pursued their goals by unlawful, unjust or extravagant means—whether against the power structure, in defense of the power structure, or against another group in the society." Extremists are not necessarily either good or bad—they just are. History is their judge.

He takes a cue from American educator Abraham Flexner: Extremists "are the gadflies that keep society from being too complacent, or self-satisfied; they are, if sound, the spearhead of progress." In one sense, this is a book about those who have been agents for change, for better or worse, throughout our history.

I love Archer's emphasis on the Bill of Rights, the first ten Amendments to our Constitution. (As the author of *A Kids' Guide to America's Bill of Rights*, 2015, I support a thorough education on the Bill of Rights.) The First Amendment guarantees our right of free speech, meaning that everyone is entitled to be an extremist, no matter how unpopular the opinion. As he mentions, the American Civil Liberties Union (ACLU) can take legal action to defend someone's right to speak his or her mind. The trick for *us,* the students of history, is to use our brains, thoughtfully evaluate both sides of an issue, and draw our own conclusions about extremism. Be informed, then make up your own mind.

It does turn out, in Archer's loose definition, that just about anyone can be called extremist. The word becomes a vehicle to tell the American story right up to one of its most extremist years, 1968.

Chapter 1 is tantalizingly titled "Ear-Slicers, Witch-hunters, and Roughnecks." In a twist you might not have seen coming, those who sliced ears were the Puritans. Fleeing intolerance in England, they sailed here and promptly installed their own brand of religious intolerance. They really hated Quakers, with cruel and bloody punishments for dissent. Puritans were at it again with the Salem witch trials, resulting in nineteen executions that particularly targeted teenage girls acting too "exuberantly." Years later, roughnecks were tough guys who worked down at the Boston waterfront, hired by the Sons of Liberty to fan the flames of the American Revolution with physical violence.

Subsequent chapters take us into the thick of the Revolution, the extremist event that broke us away from England and began a new country.

Archer goes on to cast a wide net: patriots, vigilantes, rebels, bigots of every flavor, assassins, radicals, the Ku Klux Klan, Bohemians, John Birchers, members of what we would call the lunatic fringe, the Nat Turner rebellion and other slave revolts, and high school students wearing black armbands to protest the Vietnam War. The Civil War is presented as perhaps the ultimate example of extreme extremists in action.

Archer gives the women's rights movement more attention than he usually does—attacking the patriarchal power structure fits in so well with his theme. As the author of *A Woman for President: The Story of Victoria Woodhull* (2008), I have some quibbles with his facts about Woodhull, an extremist if ever there was one. But he gets major points for including her, all but unknown in his day, and many other women throughout.

He concludes with 1968, a year of shocking assassinations, violent anti-war demonstrations, riots over African American civil rights. Many at the time were frightened at the prospect of the very "forces of law and order breaking down." Hence the need for this book, for his message that extremists have always been part of American life, for his advice to "choose, as thinking Americans, to 'keep our cool.'" Changing "obsolete attitudes" and correcting "America's domestic and foreign policy mistakes" is crucial work—but is extremism the way to go?

This book is more advanced, denser than some of his others. But it fits in perfectly with his usual themes: resisting injustice, the importance of young people, with all their idealism and energy, and the call to get involved and make a difference. As always, clearly and concisely, Archer sums up giant chunks of history. The text is illustrated and enlivened with political cartoons from the various time periods.

In a previous lifetime, I knew Archer personally and worked with him on two of his other books—*Winners and Losers: How Elections Work in America* (1984), which was a *School Library Journal* "Best Book" and a Notable Children's Trade Book in the Field of Social Studies, and then *The Incredible Sixties: The Stormy Years that Changed America* (1986), another *SLJ* "Best Book." I knew him to be a passionate idealist, always urging young people to become informed citizens.

In this dance across all of American history (except for the last forty-six years), topics for classroom discussion abound. Perhaps the most interesting: how would Jules Archer have updated his book were he still alive?

—Kathleen Krull, 2017

I

What Is Extremism?

Police in Oakland, California, clashed violently with militant students in a week of anti-draft demonstrations late in November 1967. Governor Ronald Reagan praised the police action. "The taking of alleged grievances to the streets," he declared, "can not and will not be tolerated."

The following Sunday morning at Grace Cathedral in San Francisco, the Episcopal bishop of California delivered a sermon on extremism. He criticized right-wing extremists for attacking democratic institutions. Governor Reagan, said the Right Reverend C. Kilmer Myers, sounded as though he "would like nothing better than to clobber all dissent by use of military force." At the same time the bishop castigated the militant student leader of the demonstrations, Jeff Segal, for pursuing a left-wing extremism that "ends only with a police state."

Extremists of both right and left, he warned, were "moving toward the destruction of our nation."

The question of extremism had already been raised earlier that year when black Americans, frustrated by the slow pace of the Johnson administration's anti-poverty program, began to riot in the city ghettos. Crying, "Burn, baby, burn!" they set fire to buildings and stores, then looted them. Police, the National Guard and federal troops moved into the slums with clubs, rifles, bayonets, grenade launchers, and machine guns.

In Detroit alone there were forty deaths, 2,250 injuries and four thousand arrests. Americans were appalled and frightened.

"People have been begging for years," twenty-six-year-old black high school dropout Ed Bowen explained grimly to a *Newsweek* reporter, "for a decent place to live, a job, some food, but they ain't got nothing, so they burn things down and maybe they'll get it."

But President Lyndon B. Johnson declared, "Let there be no mistake about it—the looting, arson, plunder, and pillage which have occurred are not part of a civil rights protest. That is crime—and crime must be dealt with forcefully, swiftly, certainly."

City and state officials demanded an end to extremism in protest demonstrations. Civil rights and anti-war demonstrators replied with a demand for an end to extremism in law enforcement, charging police brutality. Anti-war forces, in addition, demanded that the government end what they charged was extremism in American foreign policy—escalating the war in Vietnam, and punishing those who objected.

During that same troubled, violent year of 1967, there were also street clashes between rival groups. Black marchers demanding open housing legislation were attacked by whites opposed to Black neighbors. Administration supporters tried to break up peace demonstrations by anti-Vietnam critics.

These dire events of a single year reflect the three classic types of extremism that have accompanied most controversial developments throughout American history.

The first type of extremism occurs when a minority group feels frustrated by the government, or by the government in collaboration with powerful special interests like the military and big business. President Dwight D. Eisenhower called these interests the "military-industrial complex." Today the combination is popularly referred to as "the Establishment" or "the power structure," terms used in this book for the dominant political party and economic class of a particular era.

When a minority despairs of winning correction of real or imagined grievances by legal means, it may feel driven to use extreme measures to protest against the Establishment. The examples in 1967 were black rioters in the ghettos and antiwar demonstrators who burned draft cards or tried to interfere with draft or military procedures.

The second type of extremism arises when the power structure, outraged by the protests or illegal acts of a minority group, replies with a mass attack by police or troops; or seeks to suppress the group by harsh, punitive laws. In 1967 many blacks who were beaten, arrested, and shot had simply been innocent bystanders in the ghettos. And General Lewis B. Hershey sought to punish anti-war demonstrators by ordering draft boards to induct them into the Army.

The third type of extremism is that directed by one group of citizens against another, often by taking the law into their own hands. The 1967 examples were the clashes between black and white groups, between peace marchers and war supporters.

Who, then, can properly be labeled an extremist?

According to one dictionary definition, an extremist is "one who advocates very new and surprising, or very severe, measures; one who has advanced or radical ideas; one who goes to extremes." But the interpretation of what is very new, surprising, very severe, advanced, radical, or going to extremes is a matter of individual judgment.

A member of the John Birch Society considers himself a fine patriotic American opposed to "the extremists"—by whom he means all those opposed to a right-wing outlook.

A member of the left-wing Students for a Democratic Society sees himself as a fighter for a decent America, opposed to "the extremists"—by whom he means the Birchers, the war hawks, the CIA, the racists and other right-wing groups.

United Press International Photo

A middle-of-the-road Republican or Democrat considers himself the only respectable kind of American, equally opposed to "the extremists" on the left and the right.

For the purposes of this book, the author has viewed as extremists those in American history who pursued their goals by unlawful, unjust, or extravagant means—whether against the power structure, in defense of the power structure, or against another group in the society.

An unlawful course of conduct is usually, but not necessarily, reprehensible. Often conscience is held to be above the law. In the Nuremberg trials following World War II, for example, Nazi prisoners accused of war crimes pleaded that they had simply been obeying German laws like patriotic citizens and soldiers. The Allied judges nevertheless found them guilty for obeying extremist laws that shocked the human conscience.

To condemn all extremists flatly would be unjust to many of our most celebrated American heroes. Violent opposition to the status quo in our democracy has been part of the American way of life from earliest times.

Roger Williams and his followers were extremists when they defied the laws of the Massachusetts Bay Colony. Our Puritan forefathers were extremists when they enforced these harsh edicts; and again when they arrested and exiled the Rhode Island groups for refusing to obey them.

Washington, Jefferson, and Adams were extremists in the eyes of the legitimate British government they subverted and overthrew by an American revolution. That colonial government was also extremist in the brutal measures it used to crush its opposition.

Our pioneers who settled the West were often extremists who robbed the Indians of their lands, and massacred them when they fought back in protest. Many early settlers were extremists who fought range wars among themselves, taking the law into their own hands and murdering enemies by "vigilante justice."

To think clearly about extremists, we need to distinguish between their ideas and their tactics. We may approve the one but not the other. Even if we agreed with radicals that a Socialist America would be better, most of us would probably *not* agree with those who insisted on violent revolution as the way to achieve such a goal. Likewise, we might agree with some of the ideas of the John Birch Society. But we might nevertheless oppose those branches of the Society that try to censor school textbooks in order to force a right-wing view of history and current events on students.

Each generation produces its own crop of extremist beliefs. Some fade quickly; others persist; some continue in changed forms. In our society today there are still echoes of "ism's" from earlier periods—Puritanism, expansionism, anti-Catholicism, secessionism, socialism, anarchism, pacifism and McCarthyism.

Our founding fathers, well aware of how quickly a government may become tyrannical if its powers are not limited, wrote into the first ten amendments to the Constitution the guarantees that allow every American to disagree with, and protest against, any laws, policies, or officials of his government at the national, state, or local level.

The right to hold and advocate extremist beliefs is firmly protected by the Bill of Rights, no matter how unpopular those beliefs may be with the majority of Americans, or with any government officials. We have reason to be grateful for many stubborn extremists of the past whose ideas, denounced at first as fanatical, eventually became law.

Few of us today find anything radical about social security, child labor laws, unemployment insurance, or farm price supports. Yet the Americans who first fought for those concepts were considered wild-eyed fanatics.

Extremism tends to flourish in times of crisis. The late President John F. Kennedy observed that whenever the United

States faces serious problems with the Soviet Union, the country becomes polarized between two vocal extremes.

"Each believes," he said, "that we have only two choices: appeasement or war, suicide or surrender, humiliation or holocaust, to be either Red or dead." He was particularly critical of the radical Right: "They call for 'a man on horseback,' because they do not trust the people. They find treason in our churches, in our highest court, in our treatment of water. They equate the Democratic Party with the welfare state, the welfare state with socialism, socialism with communism."

Many Republicans were equally resentful of efforts made by the radical Left to identify them with the John Birch Society. At the Republican National Convention in San Francisco in 1964, they demanded that an anti-extremist plank be put in the Party platform. The Presidential nominee, Senator Barry Goldwater, refused. He explained why in his acceptance speech.

"I would remind you," he said, "that extremism in the defense of liberty is no vice. And let me remind you also that moderation in the pursuit of justice is no virtue."

Goldwater was decisively defeated in the subsequent election. Josh Billings, a nineteenth century American wit, had put it a little differently: "If a man is right, he can t be too radical." But the voting public is traditionally suspicious of the avowed extremist as "a man who keeps his socks up by walking on his hands." In 1939 President Franklin D. Roosevelt defined a radical as "a man with both feet firmly planted in the air." And back in the 1880s, President James A. Garfield declared, "I am trying to do two things—dare to be a radical, and not a fool; which, if I may judge by the exhibition around me, is a matter of no small difficulty!"

The popular distrust of extremists has its ironic side. When the hippies first made their appearance on the American scene, they were widely derided and denounced. A New York minister made them the subject of his sermon one Sunday.

"I daresay," he told his congregation, "that most of us good Christians would turn away with scorn from a long-haired, bearded radical in a robe who had given away everything he owned to live on the charity of others, and who went around urging people to love and live at peace with one another. Yet may I remind my fellow Christians that all of us here today are his devoted followers and admirers?"

Politically, extremists of right and left differ totally in outlook. The radical Right generally believes in free enterprise; a minimum of government regulation; a minimum of social welfare programs; curbs on labor unions; suppression of liberal or left-wing ideas; armed intervention overseas against the spread of left-wing revolutions.

The radical Left usually believes in government operation of all or most of the economy; anti-trust regulation; social welfare programs; militant labor unions; freedom of expression for all but the radical Right; support for revolutionary movements abroad, and opposition to right-wing dictatorships.

But Walter Lippman, elder statesman of the American press, has pointed out that politics can make strange bedfellows.

"If you follow the extremists," he told Walter Cronkite, CBS newscaster, "one goes 180 degrees this way, and one goes 180 degrees that way, and they meet, and they become the same thing. We've seen that all through this generation. The German Republic, which was finally overthrown by Hitler, was overthrown by a very powerful assist from the Communist Party in Germany. . . . In our own country we know plenty of people who are on the extreme right now, and who used to be on the extreme left."

Are there legal limits to political extremism?

The Supreme Court has ruled that no group, left or right, may be denied the right of free speech or activity in our democracy, except as the government can prove that it constitutes a "clear and present danger" to the nation. Allowed to function openly, extremist groups are usually far less dangerous to a nation's security than when driven underground to plan guerrilla warfare or insurrection in secret.

Tolerance of extremism has many other advantages. The freedom of discontented minorities to advocate "ism's" provides a valuable safety valve for their anger. Extremists are also useful gadflies who make people think and provoke educational discussions. Often their criticism is just and effective, compelling the government to recognize the need for reforms.

Most reforms, in fact, *are* initiated by extremists. When an ism begins to gain popularity, one of the two major political parties usually steals its program and incorporates it into the party platform. This is why the Populists, the Progressives and the Socialists never came to power nationally, for example, although many of their ideas were adapted by the Democrats under Woodrow Wilson and Franklin D. Roosevelt.

Americans don't usually think of extremists in the ranks of the leaders of industry, but the industrialists known to history as the robber barons were certainly extremists.

"The greatest factors making for communism, socialism, or anarchy among a free people are the excesses of capitalism," declared the late Supreme Court Justice Louis D. Brandeis. "The talk of the agitator does not advance socialism one step. The great captains of industry and finance . . . are the chief makers of socialism."

Many presidents have agreed that extremism in the power structure provokes radicalism on the left, and have sought to curb the robber barons of their day.

"I am in every fiber of my body a radical," declared President Theodore Roosevelt defiantly as he set about "busting the trusts." He explained: "The more we condemn unadulterated Marxian Socialism, the stouter should be our insistence on thoroughgoing social reforms."

If some of our most famous capitalists have been extremists, so have some of our most noted presidents. Polk was considered extreme for taking the country to war against Mexico; Andrew Johnson, for dismissing a cabinet member; Grant, for turning the administration over to crooked cronies; McKinley, for declaring war on Spain; Theodore Roosevelt, for grabbing the Panama Canal; Wilson, for trying to force the United States into the League of Nations; Hoover, for ordering troops out against the bonus marchers on Washington; Franklin D. Roosevelt, for trying to "stack" the Supreme Court to decide in favor of New Deal legislation; Truman, for firing America's number one war hero, General Douglas MacArthur; Kennedy, for the Bay of Pigs misadventure; Lyndon B. Johnson, for the Vietnam War.

In each case, of course, the charge of extremism represented a value judgment made by political opponents and critics. Presidents seldom think of themselves as extremists.

The charge of extremism, if it can be made to stick, is usually damaging to a public figure. Most people tend to be cautious about supporting anyone too far from the middle of the road. Walter Goodman, in his book, *All Honorable Men,* gives this picture of American thinking about extremists:

"Popular psychology conveys a feeling that the person who attracts attention—whether it is General Edwin Walker or Bertrand Russell—is emotionally suspect; active extremism, whether in favor of lynching or in favor of school integration, may be a symptom of a disordered ego; the well-balanced person plays it cool."

Time and history prove many extremist groups to be wrong in their ideas or tactics, or both. But others become esteemed, like the abolitionists who broke the law, often violently, to end slavery. On balance, it would seem an obvious mistake to denounce an ism solely because it *is* extreme.

If we do, we may find ourselves in the embarrassing position of the garrulous politician, campaigning for office, who cried out to a crowd in ringing tones, "I want you to know that I hate Communism, Socialism, atheism, Marxism—*and every other Ism in the world!*"

"What!" called out a straight-faced heckler. "Do you expect all of us here to vote for a man who comes right out and says he hates capitalism and Americanism?"

Senator William E. Borah, who considered himself a "progressive Republican," once told the Senate in 1929, "We need not take shelter when someone cries 'Radical!' If measures proposed are unsound, debate will reveal this fact better than anything else that has been discovered in the affairs of government. But if the measures are sound, we want them."

The late American educator Abraham Flexner said, "We must not overlook the important role that extremists play. They are the gadflies that keep society from being too complacent, or self-satisfied; they are, if sound, the spearhead of progress."

It would seem reasonable to suggest, therefore, that a well-informed American keeps an open mind; listens to extremists of every persuasion, left and right; weighs both sides; then draws the most intelligent conclusions he can from all the facts and arguments available for his judgment.

Everyone under our democracy has the right to be heard, and to speak his mind freely. It doesn't matter whether he is a racial or religious bigot, a black nationalist opposed to "white power," a pacifist who wants the draft ended, a jingoist who urges that H-bombs be dropped on Red China, a capitalist who wants the income tax revoked, a communist who wants socialism, or a Bircher who wants to impeach Earl Warren.

You don't have to agree with him. But the American Civil Liberties Union will go to court, if necessary, to fight for his right to speak his mind under the Bill of Rights. If he doesn't have that right, then neither do you.

This book attempts to provide a background for thoughtful evaluation of the burning issues of today, and of the many shades of extremist solutions offered for them. The chapters that follow are a cavalcade of other American times of crisis that provoked extremist movements, explaining why they arose, how they were received, and what happened to them.

2

Ear-Slicers, Witch-Hunters, and Roughnecks

To escape persecution by the Episcopalian power structure of England, on March 29, 1630, almost a thousand men, women, and children set sail in eleven ships for the New World. Arriving in Salem harbor ten weeks later, these religious dissenters known as Puritans set up their "particular church"—the Congregational—in the American wilderness.

Getting rid of Puritan leader John Winthrop and his "trouble-making" extremists was a great relief to the Church of England, which was only too happy to export another fifteen thousand religious radicals in 187 more ships to join the Massachusetts Bay Company during the next decade.

One of the first acts of these early American victims of intolerance was to draw up severe laws penalizing anybody who disagreed with *them*. Having sacrificed their homes in England and endured a desperate voyage across fearsome seas to a new and unknown land, they felt entitled to insist on absolute conformity to their own beliefs and practices. The company's charter gave them control over immigration, with "full and absolute power and authority to correct, punish, and rule."

Under Winthrop as governor, the clergy were established as the ruling class, and they made Biblical dogma the basis of civil law. These apostles of religious liberty listed eighty-two opinions that were not allowed to be held, and nine expressions that could not be used in speech. Every member of the company had to support the Puritan Congregational Church and attend services regularly; he could not vote unless he did both. Criticism of the church or colony magistrates was a criminal act.

"From the beginning, the Pilgrim Fathers were pretty intolerant," observes Britain's leading historian, Professor Arnold Toynbee. "I sometimes say Britain was being rather sly. She exported all her intolerant people to the American colonies as she exported her criminals. . . . This strain of Puritanism runs through America's history."

The extremist Puritan power structure viewed minister-teacher Roger Williams as a dangerous radical when he dared to challenge the whole premise of the Pilgrim society. "No one should be bound to maintain a worship against his consent," Williams preached in defiance of the law. He denied the right of the government to compel obedience to biblical dogma, insisting upon separation of church and state. He even denounced the company for settling land stolen from the Indians. By what right, he demanded, did the English king give away, by charter, lands in America that did not belong to England?

Arrested for "newe and dangerous opinions, against the authorise of magistrates," he was banished from the company. To avoid deportation back to England, he fled south to establish a new colony at what is now Providence, Rhode Island, where each man could worship in his own way—or not at all—and had an unqualified vote in free elections. In 1636 he founded what for that time was the most startling experiment in the world—a total democracy.

Colonists of any persuasion were welcomed—Protestants, Catholics, Quakers, Jews, and atheists. "None bee accounted a Delinquent for Doctrine," Williams insisted. He even discouraged attempts to convert indians to Christianity, considering their own religion just as valid as the white man's.

Meanwhile, in 1637 Governor Winthrop put another dissenter on trial—Mrs. Anne Hutchinson, a woman "of a haughty and fierce carriage, of nimble wit and active spirit and a very voluble tongue." Winthrop sentenced her, too, to banishment "as being a woman not fit for our society."

"Wherefore am I banished?" she demanded indignantly.

"Say no more," he replied as imperiously as a British monarch. "The court knows wherefore and is satisfied!"

Between 1656 and 1662 the Pilgrim Fathers also conducted a pogrom against Quakers, many of whom were irreverent extremists who publicly mocked the rabid Puritan laws and officials, interrupted church services, and behaved outrageously. The Establishment passed new laws which, on first conviction, cost a Quaker one ear cut off; second conviction, second ear; third conviction, the tongue bored through by a hot iron.

So much for our beginnings as "a nation under law."

The Virginia Colony also had its extremists, both in the power structure and in the populace. From 1660 to 1674 Governor William Berkeley ruled as an iron-fisted dictator. Taxing only poor farmers, for the benefit of himself and a privileged class of officials, he wielded power by the spoils system. He controlled jobs, land grants, and fur trade profits.

The plight of poor Virginia farmers became desperate in 1668 when tobacco prices plunged. To add to their troubles, Indians who resented the settlers' encroachment upon their lands began raiding farms on the unprotected western borderlands of the colony. When farmers pleaded with Governor Berkeley for protection, he ignored them. Bitter, they blamed his "love to the Beaver"—that is, his greed for profits from the Indian fur trade.

Three hundred small farmers angrily mustered themselves into a force of armed vigilantes. They asked Nathaniel Bacon, a young plantation owner, to lead them against the Indians. The governor indignantly ordered them to disband, but Bacon led them against the Occaneechees, who were actually a friendly tribe of fur traders. Bacon fired their palisades, stormed and burned their fort and cabins, and murdered 150 Indians at a cost of three white settlers' lives.

Acclaimed as a hero, he was sent to the Virginia Assembly as the representative of the border farmers. But when he sought to take his seat, Berkeley had him arrested as a rebel. An instant uprising on the border, however, forced his release. He reported back to his followers that it was useless to look for any official help against the Indians from the Establishment.

"Consider what hope there is of redress," he said, "in appealing to the very persons our complaints do accuse."

When Indian raids on the border intensified, Bacon rallied four hundred armed farmers for a march on Jamestown. News of their coming so outraged the governor that he dashed out of the Statehouse to confront them.

"Here!" he shouted furiously, tearing open his shirt and baring his naked chest. "Shoot me! Before God, a fair mark— shoot!"

Bacon and his followers were startled by this extreme behavior on the part of the supreme ruler of Virginia.

"No, may it please your honor," he stammered, "we will not hurt a hair of your head, nor any man's. We are come for a commission to save our lives from the Indians, which you have so often promised, and now we will have it before we go!"

"We *will have it!*" roared the farmers, brandishing their guns at the terrified white faces staring from the windows of the Statehouse. The settlers then stormed inside where, for half an hour, Bacon harangued the legislators. He demanded protection for the settlers, inspection of the public accounts, reduction of taxes on poor farmers, and land grants. The lawmakers, petrified by all the cocked guns surrounding them, hastily passed all the demanded legislation, including a law that gave voting rights to all freemen in the colony.

As soon as Bacon had led his extremists home in triumph, the governor promptly proclaimed him a traitor. A force of twelve hundred militia were ordered to attack the border farmers. To Berkeley's dismay they broke ranks and left the field muttering rebelliously, "Not Bacon, not Bacon, not Bacon."

Outraged by news of the governor's double-cross, Bacon sped back to Jamestown with his devoted followers. Berkeley fled with his own supporters. Re-establishing his government aboard several armed merchant ships, he controlled the coastal waterways of Virginia while Bacon and his rebels swept over the mainland. Jamestown was burned as a hated symbol of extremist power, to keep it out of Berkeley's hands.

Now master of the Virginia Colony, "General" Bacon set up his own *de facto* government. He was determined to capture Berkeley and ship him back to London to face charges of corruption, confident that the facts would vindicate his radical decision to overthrow the Virginia Establishment.

But Charles II, alarmed by the extremist "uproars" in the colony, sent an army to crush the rebellion. Frightened by this news, many followers of the twenty-eight-year-old Bacon began deserting him. In desperation, he sought to encourage the five hundred followers who remained loyal to him. "May not five hundred Virginians beat them," he urged hopefully, "we having the same advantages against the Red Coates the Indians have against us?"

But weakened by forced marches, hunger, exposure and fatigue, malaria and dysentery, Nathaniel Bacon died on October 26, 1676, even before the British Army arrived. His followers buried his body secretly so that it could not be exposed on a gibbet as Berkeley had threatened. With his death, the rebellion collapsed. Berkeley savagely hung all the extremists he could lay his hands on—a total of twenty-three.

Ironically, when the fleet finally arrived from England, it brought Charles II's pardon to the rebels, and a cold order for Berkeley to return to London and explain his dismal rule. Before the crestfallen governor arrived in England, ships preceding him brought word of his execution of Bacon's followers.

"That old fool," the king groaned to his courtiers, "has hanged more men in that naked country than I did for the murder of my father!" Perhaps fortunately for Berkeley, he died of old age in 1677, before he had to answer for his excesses.

Colonial extremism of a different sort marked the events that took place in Salem Village (now Danvers), Massachusetts, in the spring of 1692. It was a time when belief in witchcraft was worldwide, education being a very rare commodity. The penalty for witches was indicated in the one book that had widest currency, more through sermons than reading. "Thou shalt not," said Exodus 22:18, "suffer a witch to live."

Even half a century after the Salem trials, so distinguished an English jurist as William Blackstone could write, "To deny the possibility, nay, actual existence, of witchcraft and sorcery is flatly to contradict the revealed word of God."

The principals at Salem were a group of teenage girls, bored to desperation by the long New England winter of 1691–92, and eager for excitement of any kind to break the monotony. They met nightly at the parsonage of the Reverend Samuel Parris, titillated by having their fortunes told by his West Indian female servant, Tituba. She also held them spellbound by her stories about voodoo in the Islands, frightening some to the point of hysteria. They shrieked, jumped, and writhed in the kind of emotional outbursts that young girls today often manifest at performances by popular singing idols.

But to the alarmed ignorant elders of Salem Village, the "afflicted children" were victims of witchcraft. The girls were delighted by the attention they attracted, and obligingly exaggerated their emotionalism. On February 28, 1692, Tituba and two local old crones—Sarah Good and Sarah Osburn—were arrested for witchcraft. Hearings began.

Justices Corwin and Hawthorne (a relative of Nathaniel Hawthorne) confronted each defendant with the children, asking the teenagers if she was one of their "tormentors." Shrieking "Yes!" they proceeded to throw fits. The judges ordered the defendant to touch them, whereupon they promptly quieted down, proving to the court that she was, indeed, a witch. Popular belief held that a witch's touch could extract evil spirits from the afflicted.

"Do you not see what you have done?" Justice Hawthorne would demand indignantly of each defendant. "Why do you keep denying the truth? Why do you torment these poor children?"

To escape the hangman's noose, Tituba quickly agreed to turn King's evidence by pleading guilty to witchcraft and testifying luridly against the other accused witches. Sarah Good and Sarah Osburn were hanged. The thrilled Salem teens, drunk with power, now named 150 other citizens as associate witches. Incredibly, all those accused were arrested.

The new governor of the colony, Sir William Phips, appointed a special court to try the cases. Among those arrested was Captain John Alden, son of Miles Standish's famous friend. He saved himself by breaking out of jail. But thirteen men and six women went to the gallows as convicted witches.

One of the most enthusiastic supporters of the Salem trials was a leading Puritan minister, the Reverend Cotton Mather, who assured uneasy New Englanders that there was "a plot of the Devil against New England." He was enjoying one hanging when the doomed victim, a clergyman, eloquently protested his innocence to a silent crowd as his head was placed in a noose. Some spectators cried out for his release.

Mather shouted out a warning to Salemites not to be deceived. "The Devil," he cried, "has often been transformed into an Angel of Light!" The execution went as scheduled.

One accused farmer, Giles Corey, refused to plead either innocent or guilty. There was a method in his madness. The law said that a defendant who pleaded *nolo contendere* (I do not wish to contest), could not have his property confiscated by the State. His strategy insured that his heirs would inherit all his belongings. But angered magistrates punished him by ordering him killed, as the law allowed, by being crushed to death under weights and stones.

The "afflicted children" of Salem finally went too far when they named as their next witch to be tried Madam Phips, the Governor's lady. Reaction set in swiftly.

"I am afraid," admitted Boston businessman and Harvard treasurer Thomas Brattle on October 8, 1692, "that ages will not wear off that reproach and those stains which these things will leave behind them upon our land."

By 1693 the Establishment in Massachusetts had grown appalled by its own insane extremities. Justice Nathaniel Saltonstall, one of the original Salem judges, resigned rather than participate in any more witchcraft trials. Another judge, Samuel Sewall, publicly admitted "blame and shame." The Massachusetts General Court designated January 14, 1697, as a day of repentance for the nineteen legally murdered martyrs.

In 1711 indemnities were paid to all their heirs.

During the early 1700s extremists in the power structure of Connecticut passed a series of "Blue Laws." These laws, said the

Reverend Samuel A. Peters of New Haven, "betrayed such an extreme degree of wanton cruelty and oppression that even the rigid fanatics of Boston and the mad zealots of Hartford, put to the blush, christened the Blue Laws . . . bloody laws; for they were all sanctified with excommunication, confiscation, fines, banishments, whippings, cutting off of the ears, burning the tongue, and death."

Under the Blue Laws, Connecticut citizens were forbidden to cross a river except with an authorized ferryman; to run, walk in the garden, travel, cook, make beds, shave, or kiss a child on Sundays; to read Common Prayer; to make minced pie or play cards; or to live apart from a wife. Most of these laws, however, were so widely flouted that the government dared not enforce them.

The stage for a major crisis in extremism was set in 1763, when Great Britain acquired Canada from France and set about tightening up its colonial administration in North America. The middle classes of the thirteen colonies, used to self-government, resented new duties laid upon their commerce. In 1764 Parliament's Sugar Act taxed their lumber, food, molasses, and rum. A year later a Stamp Act forced them to pay taxes to support Royal troops quartered in their cities.

Outraged by these severe levies on the part of a British power structure which allowed them no voice in Parliament, colonists in seaboard cities secretly organized into patriotic societies known as the Sons of Liberty. Often disguised as workers and sailors, they led mobs to attack the homes of British officials sworn to enforce the Stamp Act. Sometimes they hired waterfront roughnecks to harass the authorities for them.

In October 1765, the Sons organized a Stamp Act Congress in New York City at which nine colonies drew up a "declaration of rights and grievances of the Colonists of America," and sent it to the king. When indignant Virginia conservatives accused

Patrick Henry of treason for his part in this extremism, he replied, "If this be treason, make the most of it!"

An alarmed Parliament repealed the Stamp Act in March 1766. But it was soon under pressure to re-assert its authority over the intemperate Americans, and in 1767 levied new taxes and import duties under the Townshend Acts.

Colonial outrage was skillfully fanned by master agitator Samuel Adams of Boston. An unsuccessful lawyer and business-man turned politician, he brilliantly earned a later description as the "Lenin of America." When Boston merchant John Hancock was arrested aboard his sloop for smuggling Spanish wine ashore without paying customs duty, it was Adams who agitated a mob into rescuing both Hancock and his sloop.

Two regiments of British troops were rushed from Halifax to Boston. They paraded through the city to martial music as Bostonians watched sullenly. Sam Adams buttonholed many citizens with pleas that they take up arms against the redcoats. In January 1770, fights broke out between mobs using clubs against the bayonets and cutlasses of the troops. One citizen was killed. Angry threats flew on both sides.

The redcoats were so poorly paid that many of them were compelled to "moonlight" on civilian jobs when off duty. This practice was greatly resented by Boston workers, who regarded the British soldiers as labor scabs. On the second of March when three privates went to a rope factory seeking jobs, they were beaten up by workers. They fled but returned with forty more "lobster backs," only to be driven off again.

On the fifth of March British sentry Hugh White was pacing off guard duty in front of the Custom House when a group of jeering boys began throwing snowballs at him. He threatened them. Moments later the square was suddenly filled with sixty men brandishing clubs, and throwing icicles and clamshells. Shouting for the guard, Private White aimed his gun at them.

"Paying the Exciseman."
This cartoon, showing patriots tormenting a tarred-and-feathered Crown agent, ridicules both the Stamp Act and the Tea Act.

"Fire!" taunted the crowd. "Fire! We *dare* you!"

Other soldiers ran out of the barracks. Fixing bayonets, they prodded the crowd back. Captain Preston, Officer of the Day, urged the mob to disperse and go home.

Church bells suddenly rang an alarm. People began running toward the Custom House square, swelling the infuriated crowd. The soldiers loaded and primed their guns. The mob pressed against their bayonets, defying them.

One soldier was clubbed to the ground. Regaining his feet he fired into the crowd. Other shots echoed his.

Screaming, the civilians fled from the square. The squad hastily retreated to barracks. Some Bostonians ran back to carry off the casualties—three dead, two injured. One of the dead men was Crispus Attucks, the first black citizen to die in the American Revolution.

Feeling ran high as Sam Adams and other Sons of Liberty extremists fanned public rage over "the Boston Massacre." He and John Hancock led a march on the Town House to demand that Colonel Dalrymple, the British commander in Boston, withdraw his four hundred troops from the city to a harbor fort. Threatened with war by fifteen thousand armed Bostonians, Dalrymple hastily agreed.

The Boston extremists were playing for bigger stakes than just driving four hundred redcoats out of their city.

3

The Extremists of 1776

The Sons of Liberty staged an elaborate, highly emotional funeral for the three victims of the Boston Massacre, bells tolling solemnly as the cortege wound slowly through streets lined with thousands of grim Bostonians. They flooded the colonies with engravings by silversmith Paul Revere showing a grinning British officer waving his sword to signal a point-blank volley of redcoat rifle fire at twenty peaceful, respectable citizens. In *A Short Narrative of the Horrid Massacre in Boston*, Sam Adams whipped up revolutionary fervor with a lurid, highly colored account of the extremist brawl.

A calmer appraisal of the affair appeared merely as a footnote in a British book published ten years later, *An Impartial History of the War in America*, mentioning it as "an alarming riot in Boston between the soldiers and the inhabitants." But each year until the revolution proper began, the Sons held a Fifth of March demonstration to remind colonists of their first martyrs—the dockworkers and street toughs who had provoked the riot in King Street, instigated, many thought, by Sam Adams.

Colonial extremism provoked counter-extremism in the British Establishment. Perhaps its most reasonable member was Lord William Pitt, who persuaded Parliament to repeal the Townshend Acts and declared, "I love the Americans because they love liberty." But he also added sternly, "They must be subordinate...."

In all laws relating to trade and navigation especially, this is the mother country, they are the children; they must obey, and we prescribe." Extremists never compromise.

Nor did Sam Adams. He kept inflaming anti-British sentiment by such demagoguery as reporting in the Boston *Gazette* that he had seen dogs "greedily licking human blood in King Street." He also sought to unify Sons of Liberty branches in the colonies by establishing "committees of correspondence," through which local grievances could be magnified nationally.

This "band of brothers, which no forge can break, no enemy destroy," provided the first crude federated structure of the colonies that was eventually to develop into the United States of America—a creation of extremists.

The next opportunity of the Sons of Liberty to whip up revolutionary fervor came with the *Gaspee* affair. In June 1772, the Crown's revenue cutter *Gaspee* ran aground on a sandspit near Providence while chasing a smuggler. A merchant named John Brown quickly rounded up sixty-four extremists, and they rowed out to the *Gaspee* in longboats. Swarming over the beached cutter, they wounded the captain, fought and captured the crew, and set the ship afire. It blew up and sank.

An outraged Britannia, which presumably ruled the waves, offered large rewards for apprehension of the American pirates. John Brown was arrested, but had to be released when no witnesses could be found to testify against him. The Sons of Liberty spread rumors that *Gaspee* suspects were going to be shipped to England to stand trial. When Sam Adams joyfully relayed this unfounded propaganda through the network of committees of correspondence, holdout Colonies joined up in indignation.

A worried British Parliament repealed the irksome Townshend Acts, except for a tax on tea retained in the desperate hope of reminding Americans that they were still British subjects. The tax was significant because the Americans were still British enough to esteem tea breaks several times a day, as well as with meals. Many Americans sought to thwart the tea tax by buying only contraband tea brought in by smugglers.

In May 1773, the British East India Tea Company found itself in difficult straits—long on tea, short of cash. The British ministry obligingly granted it a monopoly in the American market. It was allowed to sell directly to colonial retailers, bypassing the wholesalers, at low prices that even with the tea tax made it cheaper than smugglers' imports.

American smugglers and wholesalers were outraged. Many switched from Tories to Whig radicals in protest. But they were faced with a difficult problem—how did you convince colonists who have been offered cheaper tea that they didn't want it? Anti-British extremist Sam Adams had the solution for them. Let tea be viewed symbolically—as a symbol of royal arrogance!

He warned Americans that if they did not "show the King" at every port where tea was landed, they "would drink themselves out of their liberties." In Charleston mobs forced tea imports to be locked in a damp warehouse; at Philadelphia and New York tea ship captains were turned back to England.

When three tea ships arrived in Boston harbor on December 16, 1773, Sam Adams himself led a boarding party of fifty men disguised as Mohawk Native Americans and black men. Bursting open 343 chests of tea, they dumped them into the harbor. The ebbing tide smothered the sea from Boston to Dorchester in a surface of fine tea shipped from India at great cost.

Sam Adams's defiant "Boston Tea Party" thrilled colonists throughout America. But his act of extremism infuriated the Crown. If rebellious Boston was not punished, the king and Parliament were convinced, then other colonies would quickly decide to challenge British power. So the port of Boston was closed to all commerce. The military commander, General Thomas Gage, was appointed governor of Massachusetts, with

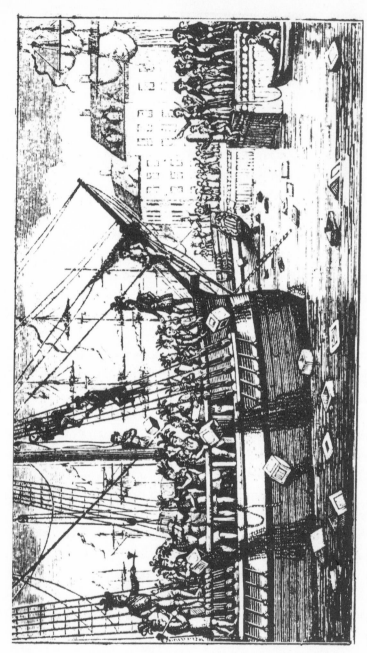

The Boston Tea Party roused a patriotic fervor in colonists throughout America.

Bostonians forced to quarter his troops. Elected officials of the colony were replaced by appointees. Boston was replaced by Salem as the colony's capital. "The die is now cast," the king wrote his prime minister, Lord North. "The Colonies must either submit or triumph." He did not have to wait long for his answer.

The Sons of Liberty promptly labeled his extremist reactions "the Intolerable Acts." Spurred by Sam Adams's rabble-rousing, the committees of correspondence called a 1774 Continental Congress of fifty-three delegates from all colonies except Georgia. Adams whipped them to a point of hysteria over Britain's Quebec Act, which extended Quebec's boundaries southward, and guaranteed French Canadians the right to be Catholics. He alarmed delegates with dark hints of George III's "popery," charging a conspiracy "establishing the Roman Catholic religion" in Canada, and "erecting a tyranny there to the great danger . . . of the neighboring British colonies."

Passion swiftly replaced reason on both sides of the Atlantic. Voices of moderation were drowned in a rising crackle of gunfire. When Governor Gage dissolved the Massachusetts Bay Colony Assembly, colonists defied him by meeting at Concord as a provincial congress. Collecting arms and ammunition, they created a militia of "minutemen" to fight instantly if Gage's redcoats moved out of Boston to attack them.

Sam Adams and John Hancock were declared outlaws with a price on their heads, and hid out in Lexington. On April 18, 1775, Gage sent troops to Concord to destroy the Rebels' munition dumps. Silversmith Paul Revere, one of a group of Boston spies for the conspirators, galloped off on his famous midnight ride through the countryside to arouse sleeping Rebels.

When the redcoat Major John Pitcairn reached Concord with his troops, he found his way barred by a line of some sixty sullen-faced minutemen with muskets. Seconds earlier Paul

Revere had passed through their line hearing their commander, Captain John Parker, order, "Let the troops pass by, and don't molest them, without they begin first."

Now Pitcairn shouted, "Disperse, ye rebels, disperse!"

A defiant shot rang out from behind a stone wall.

Those words and that shot touched off the American Revolution. Shouting and firing, the redcoats charged—"so wild they could hear no orders," a witness later related. The minutemen fled, leaping over the stone wall, but eight were killed and ten wounded. British casualties were only one leg wound and some shot in Major Pitcairn's horse.

Disdainful of the "rabble," Pitcairn marched his men on to Concord. But here, as Emerson wrote later, "the embattled farmers stood, and fired the shot heard round the world."

Fighting from cover, the minutemen killed seventy-three redcoats and wounded two hundred more, at a cost of forty-one dead and thirty-six wounded.

A gloomy King George III mulled over two contradictory reports—one from Benjamin Franklin, serving as the Rebels' agent in London, and one from General Gage. But the question of blame was now superfluous. The extremists of both sides had had their way, and a full-scale war was inevitable.

Typical of the Rebel extremists was a colorful New Englander, Ethan Allen, leader of a band of "Green Mountain Boys" dedicated to splitting off Vermont from New York. Learning that the Rebels needed cannon urgently, he led eighty-three rugged Vermont woodsmen in a surprise attack on Fort Ticonderoga on Lake Champlain. Sweeping aside a sentry who lunged at him with a bayonet, he raced to the garrison commander's quarters.

"Come out of there, you old rat!" he yelled. When an astonished officer appeared in nightclothes, Allen pointed his sword imperiously. "Surrender the garrison!"

"By whose authority?"

"In the name of the great Jehovah—and the Continental Congress!" One historian wryly noted later that the melodramatic Vermonter held no commission from either source.

But the artillery he seized was incredibly hauled to Boston on sleds across the Green and White Mountains, and less than a year later helped Washington force the British to evacuate Boston. A popular hero, Allen later fell from favor when his extremism carried him to the opposite swing of the pendulum. He was captured during a disastrous attack on Montreal, and freed two years later in a prisoner exchange.

By then he had, oddly, turned his coat, and sought to negotiate a separate treaty with England to make Vermont a British province. Another extremist who had raided Ticonderoga at his side also became famous for turning against the Revolution—Benedict Arnold, who rose to the rank of major general.

After he was made occupation commander of Philadelphia, Arnold fell in with well-to-do families of Loyalist sympathies. Charged with misconduct and profiteering, he faced a court-martial that acquitted but reprimanded him. Furious at this "insult," he conspired with British spy Major John Andre to betray American plans, and was commissioned as a Loyalist brigadier general. To vent his spite against the Rebels further, when he raided and took Fort Griswold, New London, in 1781, he massacred its defenders; he also led an expedition to burn Richmond.

When he fled to London in December 1781, he found to his dismay that the British despised him even more than the fellow Americans he had betrayed. Worn out by depression and a nervous disorder, he died embittered in 1801.

American Loyalists, whose principal crime was that they wished to remain law-respecting citizens of the government—often even when they sympathized with Rebel grievances—were early victims of intolerance and extremism.

One Boston mob tarred and feathered a group of Loyalists on suspicion of being British informers. "Several, and among them, gentlemen, were carried on rails," a Boston preacher named Shenkirk wrote in his diary in 1776. "Some were stripped naked and dreadfully abused."

The Sons of Liberty led frequent raids against the homes of Loyalist officials and sympathizers. In Wilks County, Georgia, a frontier wife named Nancy Hart, who drank, swore, and was a crack shot, often joined raids by local Sons in place of her timid husband. Once while he was away the Hart cabin was suddenly invaded by a group of angry Loyalists. Nancy was ordered to provide food and drink while they debated her punishment. She kept their cups filled until they were too tipsy to notice her ten-year-old daughter slipping off to get help.

Meanwhile Nancy, her back turned at her stove, managed to dislodge pine filling between the logs. She began slipping the men's guns through the chinks to disarm them against the rescue party she hoped would arrive. They caught her at it and two Loyalists lurched toward her. Swinging one gun up, she shot the first man, then snatched another gun and killed the second.

Seizing a third weapon, she yelled, "D_____ your Tory carcasses, surrender!" They dove for shelter. The door flew open and some Sons of Liberty came to her "rescue," her husband among them. "Shoot them all!" he squeaked wrathfully.

"No," Nancy said calmly. "Shootin's too good for d_____ Tories. Take em out and hang em!" So they were hanged.

Embittered local Loyalists called Nancy a "hellcat." The Sons of Liberty called her "a honey of a patriot."

Clashes between Loyalists and Rebels were often marked by savagery on both sides. In July 1778, Colonel John Butler led four hundred Loyalists and five hundred Seneca Indians into beautiful Wyoming Valley in Pennsylvania, where they burned and plundered a thousand homes, killing three hundred peaceful farmers who were known to support the Rebel cause.

Some of the Senecas were caught and killed by Rebels with the First New Jersey Regiment. Reported Lieutenant William Barton with obvious delight, "They skinned two of them from their hips down for boot legs, one pair for the major, the other for me."

The most important extremist of the Revolution was probably Thomas Paine, the writer-editor whose persistent campaign for American independence all through 1775 shocked George Washington. Such subversion, Washington wrote, was opposed "by any thinking man in all North America." Even after Lexington and Concord, the leaders of American dissent were asking not independence but only a greater measure of self-government.

Extremists like Sam Adams and Tom Paine were eager for rebellion, but the average American was just as alarmed by the idea of revolution as he is today. It took an incendiary pamphlet by Paine, called *Common Sense,* to fan the spark of dissatisfaction into the flame of open revolt.

For "a Continent to be perpetually governed by an island" was absurd, Paine insisted. And how could Americans continue to think themselves loyal to the Crown while already fighting the King's troops on American soil? By declaring independence instead, they would have the help of France in their fight for freedom. Paine's arguments deeply impressed Americans.

"I find *Common Sense* is working a powerful change . . . in the minds of many men," Washington was compelled to admit in April 1776. Two months later the Continental Congress ordered the drafting of a Declaration of Independence. Thomas Jefferson, after consulting with Paine, drew up the eloquent but exaggerated bill of wrongs justifying revolution.

To keep up the patriotic fervor of the ragged, often hungry and frozen Rebels who straggled in Washington's ranks, Paine wrote a series of "pep talks" called *The Crisis.* A new one would appear each time they met with serious reverses, and would be read aloud by an officer or non-com to hearten them.

Crisis I appeared when the Americans had been forced to retreat across the Delaware. "These are the times that try men's souls," Paine exhorted. "The summer soldier and the sunshine patriot will, in this crisis, shrink from the service of his country, but he that stands it NOW, deserves the love and thanks of men and women. . . . Tyranny, like hell, is not easily conquered; yet . . . the harder the conflict, the more glorious the triumph." His words were read to the troops on the shores of the Delaware at dusk just as Washington prepared to re-cross and attack the British at Trenton. Inspired by Paine, they fought brilliantly and won the first major victory of the war.

It was Paine who first used the expression "the United States of America," and who first urged that a Constitutional Convention be called in Philadelphia after victory. But he was denied a role in the new American government by powerful enemies he had made when he attacked war profiteers.

Paine was in England on private business when the French Revolution broke out. He outraged Prime Minister William Pitt by acclaiming the overthrow of the French monarchy as a good example for the British people. He escaped to France two jumps ahead of the London police. The National Convention in Paris gave him a standing ovation as a revolutionary hero.

But Paine made the mistake of aligning himself with the idealistic Girondists instead of the bloodthirsty Jacobins. During the Reign of Terror he was flung into prison. His letters of appeal to George Washington went ignored, primarily because his new book, *The Age of Reason,* was a devastating attack on organized religion and church dogma. Appearing in America early in 1794, it provoked an immediate outcry against Paine as a heretic, blasphemer, and atheist.

The first American President was too cautious and conservative to risk his own reputation by asking the French to free Paine, who was finally released through the independent efforts of the new minister to France, James Monroe. Returning home embittered, Paine openly attacked Washington as a "hypocrite in public life" for failing to help the patriot who had been so great a help to him in winning the Revolution.

Paine's enemies denounced him as a "loathesome reptile" and a "lying, drunken, brutal infidel." In 1802, however, a new President, Thomas Jefferson, invited the celebrated extremist to the White House as an honored guest. "Let Jefferson and his blasphemous crony," roared the Federalist press, "dangle from the same gallows!" Paine was cursed and jeered at by street mobs, denied transportation by stagecoach owners, excoriated from every pulpit, vilified in the press.

He died miserably in 1809, an extremist whose talent for inspiring opposition to tyranny had helped Americans mount and win their Revolution, even though they had finally turned against him for refusing to swerve from his fanatical determination to denounce what he considered injustice and hypocrisy.

In fairness to Paine as an important Revolutionary patriot who is often largely ignored in textbooks because of the controversy he provoked, it should be noted that some modern historians consider his attacks on Washington to have been not entirely without justification. And modern theologians and ministers have demanded church reforms far more radical than any Tom Paine—who was *not* an atheist—dared to suggest in his time.

4

"March with Me into the Towns!"

When the victorious American army disbanded in 1783, return-ing soldiers were shocked to find that the country they had lib-erated was firmly in the grip of war profiteers. Paid off in paper money "not worth a Continental," farmers had to pay $1,600 for a barrel of flour. State legislatures imposed heavy taxes upon them to pay off wartime obligations to wealthy speculators. Farmers who went into debt had their homes and lands seized, were thrown into jail, and when they came out were forced to "work off" what they still owed.

"Is *this* what we fought for?" disillusioned veterans asked each other. "By God, it was better under the King!"

By 1786 Massachusetts was swept by protest meetings demanding relief for debtors. But the conservative legislature, dominated by seaboard merchants, insisted that "a bargain's a bargain and must be made good." Even Sam Adams, that one-time firebrand of the Sons of Liberty turned respectable, growled that the protest meetings were the work of British secret agents out to wreck the new Republic by stirring revolt. He proposed hanging for troublemakers such as he had been.

But farmers rallied angrily behind a popular veteran, Cap-tain Daniel Shays. In order to buy food for his family, Shays had been forced to sell a magnificent sword presented to him for bravery in action by the Marquis de Lafayette.

"Tom Paine told us a lot about the rights of man we were fighting for," he said at a huge rally. "Well, the war's over—and where are those rights? Our people are being drummed into court and jailed. We petitioned for relief, but the State Legislature is deaf. All right, I say we make our *own* laws! March with me into the towns and we'll close the courts. If they can't try us farmers, they can't send any more of us to jail. Citizens, are you with me?"

With a deafening roar of approval, twelve hundred farmers took up whatever weapons they had—guns, knives, swords, clubs and horsewhips—and followed Shays in attacking the courts of county after county. They often prevented a court from sitting by tossing the judge into the streets and locking the courtroom. Then they broke open the jail and freed its prisoners.

The news shook leaders of the republic. The president of the Continental Congress was so frightened that he wrote secretly to Prince Henry of Prussia, asking if he were interested in becoming king of the United States on condition that he guarantee to suppress the revolt of the veteran extremists.

From Mt. Vernon, Washington wrote his Secretary of War, General Henry Knox, "For God's sake, tell me, what is the cause of these commotions. If they have *real* grievances, redress them if possible. If they have not, employ the force of government against them at once." Knox's reply labeled Shays and his men as an eighteenth century equivalent of Communists.

"Their creed," he wrote, "is that the property of the United States has been protected from the confiscation of Britain by the joint exertions of all, and therefore ought to be the common property of all!" He added indignantly that they had shocked "every man of principle and property in New England." That was enough for Washington, who urged swift suppression of the

Culver Pictures, Inc.
Borrowing some of their tactics from the Boston Tea Party, the participants in Shays' Rebellion demanded greater post-Revolutionary War rights.

extremists. "There are combustibles in every state," he warned, "which a spark might set a fire in."

Thomas Jefferson, now American minister to France, thoroughly disagreed. "I hold that a little rebellion now and then is a good thing," he declared. "The tree of liberty must be refreshed from time to time with the blood of patriots and tyrants. It is its natural manure."

But Establishment extremists had the upper hand. In September 1876, conservative Governor James Bowdoin of Massachusetts ordered the militia to disperse the Shays rebels and arrest their leaders for treason. Shays replied by attacking Springfield, both to seize arms from the federal arsenal and to prevent the Massachusetts Supreme Court from sitting.

Militia led by Major General Shepard fired two warning volleys of artillery over their heads. But Shays's men took the overshot as a signal that they were only being offered token resistance. Yelling and laughing, they advanced straight into a direct third volley of shot that killed three and wounded one. Shocked and dismayed, they fled into the hills.

Four months later the Massachusetts Legislature sent an entire army under General Benjamin Lincoln to mop up the Shays forces, by now reduced to pitiful resistance with staves and pitchforks. Shays fled to Vermont, and many of his followers were taken prisoner. Fourteen were sentenced to death.

But popular indignation elected a new Legislature sympathetic with their grievances. The condemned men were either pardoned or given short jail terms. Shays, too, was pardoned and allowed to return home. The desperation of his extremist movement, it turned out, had shocked Americans into realizing that something was seriously wrong.

"These disorders are evident marks of a defective government," Washington wrote the Marquis de Lafayette on March 25, 1787. "Indeed the thinking people of this country are now so well satisfied of this fact that most of the legislatures have appointed . . . delegates to meet at Philadelphia . . . to revise and correct the defects of the federal system."

This Constitutional Congress strengthened the feeble Articles of Confederation with a new strong national Constitution that would guarantee both federal justice and order.

Seven years later the new Republic faced another extremist rebellion. A 1791 act of Congress had levied a moderate excise tax of nine cents a gallon on all distilled spirits. But most of the 2,600 registered distilleries were small farm operations. Whisky stills allowed the farmers of western Pennsylvania, who had no other means of getting surplus grain across the mountains to market, to sell their surplus corn as liquor.

In 1794 they revolted against the tax in a "Whisky Rebellion" that had some support among clergymen who were either sympathizers, customers, or distillers themselves. The Reverend Nathan Strong, pastor of the First Church of Hartford, operated a distillery "within sixty rods of his church"; the Reverend Leonard Woods of Andover Theological Seminary acknowledged knowing at least forty ministers who were addicted to drinking.

When government revenue agents sought to enforce the whisky tax, Pennsylvania mobs tarred and feathered some, and drove the rest off. They threatened the government garrison in Pittsburgh, forcing Washington to call out fifteen thousand state militia.

Extremists urged the whisky farmers to secede from both Pennsylvania and the Union. But their champion in Congress, Senator Albert Gallatin, persuaded them to submit without bloodshed. Of eighteen men brought to Philadelphia for trial, only two were convicted, and Washington pardoned them both.

Like the Shays' Rebellion, the Whisky Rebellion had important political reverberations. Anti-Federalists who followed

Jefferson accused Hamilton's Federalists of an extremist reaction to a local riot. The riot had just been a pretext, they charged, for establishing federal authority over the states. When the Jeffersonians came to power in 1801, they repealed the excise tax, and whiskey went tax-free for another sixty years.

The fight of federal power versus state rights, sparked by the Whisky Rebellion, was to run like a bright red thread through the Civil War and even a hundred years later in the civil rights struggle between Washington and the South. The Whisky Rebellion also foreshadowed the lawlessness of the Prohibition era of the 1920s, when the government once again sought to interfere with the right of citizens to buy and sell spirits.

When Britain and France went to war with each other in 1793, American feelings were split between French sympathizers led by Jefferson, and British sympathizers led by Hamilton. Hoping to keep the weak new Republic from being dragged into the fracas, Washington sent John Jay to London to negotiate an Anglo-American treaty.

Jefferson angrily labeled the Jay Treaty "an infamous act." Jay was burned in effigy from one end of the nation to the other, and denounced as a "conniver at a creeping aristocracy." When Hamilton tried to defend the treaty with a balcony speech in New York City, he was stoned by an angry mob. Blood streaming from his face, he told them coldly, "If you use such knockdown arguments, I must retire." Only Washington's personal prestige won grudging Senate approval for the treaty.

French Foreign Minister Marquis de Tallyrand warned grimly that his nation might now feel compelled to seize American ships on the high seas. He hinted, however, that a ten million dollar loan to France, plus a personal bribe for himself, might be a sufficient inducement to respect American neutrality.

"Millions for defense, but not one cent for tribute!" indignantly replied United States Minister to France Charles Pinckney.

The Federalist administration of John Adams quickly rammed through Congress the Alien and Sedition Acts, allegedly aimed against French spies. It kept aliens from becoming citizens for fourteen years, empowered the President to deport or jail any "dangerous" alien, and provided fines or imprisonment for "false, scandalous or malicious" criticism of any government official. Alarmed Jeffersonian Republicans branded this extremist legislation a clear violation of the Bill of Rights, intended to cut down the vote of anti-Federalist French and Irish immigrants, and silence criticism of the administration.

When Congressman Matthew Lyon of Vermont called Adams a democracy-scorning aristocrat with an extremist foreign policy, he was arrested, fined a thousand dollars and sent to jail for four months. For denouncing his political persecution, Vermont's Anthony Haswell was fined two hundred dollars and imprisoned for two months.

Jefferson and Madison had had enough. Jefferson wrote the Kentucky Resolutions and Madison the Virginia Resolutions, both declaring the Alien and Sedition Acts null and void because they violated the Constitution's guarantees of free speech and free press. It was the first direct defiance of federal power by the States.

Hoodlum gangs took their cue from the extremism of the Establishment. They dragged anti-Federalist editors out of bed in the middle of the night and smashed their presses. Americans who referred to the Bill of Rights were denounced as advocates of sedition, attacked and persecuted. Adams' supporters in Congress even proposed a bill making it an act of treason to speak against the Sedition Law. Federalist judges raged at any lawyer who dared defend a victim of the Sedition Law in court as "a traitor to his country."

Adams coldly refused to heed Hamilton's plea for moderation and repeal of the Acts, and they fell out. Vice President

Thomas Jefferson felt that he could no longer remain within the ranks of a party that he felt Adams had turned into a coterie of aristocratic fanatics. He broke away to establish a new party of Democratic-Republicans, appealing to the broad masses of small farmers, workers and shopkeepers.

Enraged Federalists abused Jefferson as an atheistic agent of the French Revolution. Hoodlum gangs were sent to sing jeering and threatening songs under his window. To escape open insults by Federalist extremists, he was compelled to retire from Washington's social circles.

But by 1800 Americans had had enough of Adams's rabid administration of "the rich, the well-born and the able," and Jefferson was elected President. The oppressive Alien and Sedition Laws instantly became dead letters, and their victims were released from prison. Jefferson's election frightened New England Federalists, who were terrified that the national pendulum would now swing to the opposite extreme with a French-style reign of terror against the rich and the clergy.

"Must we with folded hands wait for the result?" cried Senator Timothy Pickering of Massachusetts. "The principles of our revolution point to the remedy—a separation!"

He and other extremist leaders of New England secretly plotted to secede and set up a Northern Confederacy of New England and New York. To gain control of New York they put forth as their candidate Aaron Burr, who had already served the state as a senator and as the attorney general. An ambitious man, Burr had been bitterly disappointed when a single electoral vote (influenced by Hamilton) had made Jefferson President in 1800, forcing him into second place as Vice President.

His pride had been hurt when Jefferson not only ignored him in office, but also dropped him from the Democratic-Republican ticket in the 1804 elections. He was only too willing, therefore, to switch party labels and run for New York Governor on the Federalist ticket. The schemers promised that if he won and pulled New York out of the Union, he would be made President of the new Northern Confederacy.

Word of this extremist plot reached the ears of Alexander Hamilton, and he denounced it publicly. Burr was trounced in the New York elections. Twice frustrated by Hamilton, Burr found a pretext for forcing him into a duel and killed him. A public outcry forced Burr to flee to the West, where he became embroiled in new extremist schemes. One involved raising a small army to capture New Orleans and rule it as a British protectorate. Another called for "liberating" Mexico from Spain with himself as emperor. But a fellow conspirator, General James Wilkinson, betrayed him.

On Jefferson's orders he was arrested for treason and tried in a Richmond, Virginia, court. Acquitted for lack of evidence, Burr prudently left for the France of Napoleon. Here he raised funds for such mad projects as restoring Canada to France, and collecting an army of unemployed Americans to march on Washington and set himself up as a dictator. But when he returned to New York in 1812, it was only to open a law firm, marry a rich widow, squander her fortune, and die in obscurity.

When Jefferson left office in 1809, his successor, James Madison, faced ominous problems growing out of the Napoleonic Wars. France and England were each trying to compel Americans to support its own side—Napoleon by threatening to confiscate neutral ships trading with Britain, the English by taxing neutral shipping. They were also arrogantly boarding foreign ships and impressing kidnapped seamen into the British Navy. An astonishing total of six thousand American sailors were enslaved by this official piracy on the high seas.

Jefferson had sought to avoid embroilment by passing the Embargo Act of 1807, prohibiting commerce with other nations.

But angry protests from New England manufacturers had forced him to replace it with the Non-Intercourse Act of 1809, embargoing trade only with Britain and France. One year later Madison lifted the embargo against France when Napoleon promised to let American shipping alone. The British reluctantly followed France's example on June 23, 1812.

But unknown to them, because of the slowness of sea communications, the United States had already declared war on England five days earlier. Who wanted the War of 1812 and why?

The War Hawks, as they were known even then, were mostly extremists from the West and frontier South—men like Henry Clay of Kentucky and John Calhoun of South Carolina. They controlled the Twelfth Congress of 1811–13. War with England appealed to them as a chance to grab rich farmlands from Canada, and forest lands from British-controlled Indian tribes on the Western frontier. So they stirred a war vote with ringing speeches about the need to protect America's "national honor."

John Randolph of Virginia urged Congress to vote down the War Hawks. Was the United States, he demanded, to remain at peace with "barbarians and savages of every clime and color," but to go to war against "those whose blood flows in our veins; in common with whom we claim Shakespeare . . . whose government is the freest on earth, our own only excepted?" If they defeated Britain, Napoleon would become the greatest naval power. How safe, he challenged, would the United States be *then*?

When the War Hawks carried the day, the pro-British Federalists of New England were appalled. The government of Massachusetts issued a manifesto calling for a peace party, urging, "Let there be no volunteers for a war against England." Connecticut and Rhode Island joined it in declining to call up the state militia for national duty. Federalist merchants refused to buy war bonds or furnish privateers for war.

Counter-extremism broke out in Baltimore. A mob smashed the newspaper plant of a Federalist editor who came out for peace, forcing him to seek refuge in the city jail with two friends, both generals. The mob broke into the jail and dragged them out. All three were beaten unmercifully, and one general was killed. The outrage turned Marylanders against the Democratic-Republicans, and the state went Federalist.

After two and a half dreary years of an indecisive war, the convention of New England delegates met at Hartford to denounce it. They threatened secession if the administration persisted in continuing the conflict. Nine days later the Treaty of Ghent brought the war to an inconclusive close.

Having at least won the right to sail the seas without paying tribute to the British Navy, Madison also determined to stop the blackmailing of United States merchant vessels by the Barbary powers who operated pirate corsairs out of North Africa. In 1815 Commodore Stephen Decatur was sent to the Mediterranean with a squadron of ten warships. Defeating the Algerian fleet, he exacted a protective treaty and sailed home in triumph.

The Navy town of Norfolk, Virginia, threw a banquet in his honor. The toasts were extravagantly boastful: "The Mediterranean ! The sea not more of Greek and Roman, than of American glory!" And, "The [Moslem] crescent! Our stars have dimmed its luster!" Decatur responded with an historic toast.

"Our country!" he proposed. "In her Intercourse with foreign nations, may she always be in the right . . . but our country, right or wrong!" This last phrase became the watchword of the American military, patriotic societies, and the radical Right. It expresses the sincere convictions of extremists that when an administration becomes involved in a war, it amounts to treason to criticize the administration's judgment, or question whether the war is a just one. They believe that once Americans are fighting beyond the nation's borders, patriotism requires all citizens to give them and the war total support.

Extremists on the opposite side take a cynical view of what they consider flag-waving, believing with Dr. Samuel Johnson, "Patriotism is the last refuge of a scoundrel." Liberals and the radical Left of 1846 attacked the Polk administration for raising the Decatur motto to silence bitter critics of the Mexican War. Author James Russell Lowell called it scathingly, "that pernicious sentiment, 'Our country, right or wrong.'"

In 1872 Senator Carl Schurz offered a substitute toast still popular with intellectual dissenters today: "Our country, right or wrong! When right, to be kept right; when wrong, to be put right!" A wry and witty comment on Decatur's motto came from British writer G. K. Chesterton, who said, " 'My country, right or wrong,' is a thing that no patriot would think of saying except in a desperate case. It is like saying, 'My mother, drunk or sober!'"

The controversy, still a burning one in 1968, flamed highest in the bitter argument between extremists of left and right over the issue of American involvement in Vietnam.

5

Mob Hysteria Against Masons and Catholics

In the view of Fisher Ames, ultra-aristocratic spokesman for the Federalists, Jefferson—a Virginia gentleman who should have known better—had opened America to rule by rabble. As Thomas Jefferson's pressure compelled more and more states to drop property qualifications for voting, government by "gentlemen" began giving way to government by the common man.

"Of all governments, the worst is that which never fails to excite . . . passions, that is, democracy," Ames wrote with a shudder. He added, "Democracy is the creature of impulse and violence . . . the vileness and cruelty of men are displayed with surprising uniformity." If Ames had not died in 1808, the shock of Andrew Jackson's inauguration twenty-one years later would surely have killed him. It was unique in American history.

The poor masses who made up the bulk of Americans were overjoyed when one of their own, a former frontiersman born in a log cabin, was elevated to the Presidency and rode to his inauguration on horseback instead of in a splendid carriage.

Storming into Washington by the thousands, they crashed the White House reception.

Standing on costly damask-covered chairs with muddy boots, they cheered their hero wildly. Many rushed forward to pump his hand, elbowing the rich and fashionable to one side. People shoved, scrambled, fought, romped. Women fainted; men got bloody noses; clothing was torn; expensive glass and china went splintering against walls and floors. A dazed Daniel Webster stammered, "I never saw anything like it before!"

A Washington society woman, Mrs. Margaret Bayard Smith, wrote in outrage, "What a pity what a pity! . . . the whole house had been inundated by the rabble mob. . . . The President, after having been *literally* pressed to death and almost suffocated and torn to pieces in their eagerness to shake hands with Old Hickory, had retreated through the back way and had escaped to his lodgings. . . . Those who got in could not get out by the door again, but had to scramble out of windows."

The mobs were finally lured out of the White House by tubs of punch planted on the front lawn for twenty thousand people.

Jackson soon proved that he could be just as passionate on behalf of the common man as the latter was on behalf of Old Hickory. In 1832 a delegation of the nation's most eminent bankers called at the White House to demand renewal of the government charter of the Bank of the United States. That charter gave the corporation a monopoly of financial power.

"You are a den of vipers and thieves," Jackson snarled at them. "I intend to rout you out, and by the eternal God, I *will* rout you out!" He not only vetoed renewal of the bank charter, but won a second term by appealing to popular prejudice against the rich. Much of his support came from naturalized immigrants who saw in Jackson's Democratic Party a champion of the poor against the powerful.

The Democrats insisted upon the rights of workers to organize; called for a ten-hour limit to the workday; asked for a secret ballot; and demanded protection for religious minorities, as well as total freedom of expression.

"Radicals!" fumed conservative, native-born Americans. They built a new Whig Party of opposition on the ashes of the dead and discredited Federalists.

Whig extremists became ringleaders of an hysterical movement directed against the fraternal order of Freemasons, an international society dedicated to religious toleration and the basic equality of men. Its members had included such famous Americans as Washington and Ben Franklin. Hostility toward the Masons was whipped up by blaming them as the conspiratorial power behind the French Revolution, which Democrats from Jefferson to Jackson were charged with having used as their model for an American "mobocracy."

The anti-Masonic movement exploded in 1826. William Morgan, a tailor and disgruntled Mason of Batavia, New York, was suddenly kidnapped after announcing that he was writing a book to "expose" Masonic secrets. Lured or forced into a carriage and spirited off to Fort Niagara, he was never seen again.

Whig papers led the uproar. "It is no uncommon thing," noted *Niles' Weekly Register* on March 24, 1827, "so great is the excitement, to find from five to six columns in one New York newspaper about it." The Whigs charged that Morgan had been murdered on the order of Masonry to stop him from exposing their "blasphemous and conspiratorial secrets."

Whigs were quick to remind voters that those staunch Democrats, Andrew Jackson and DeWitt Clinton, Governor of New York, were both Masons of high degree. Many known Masons were defeated for public office; some in office were fired on the ground that their secret oaths as Masons violated their oaths of public trust. Masonic merchants were boycotted; Masonic ministers were driven out of their pulpits by their congregations.

Alarmed, Governor Clinton offered a reward for anyone who could clear up the mystery of the Morgan case. Several suspects were finally arrested on charges of abducting the missing tailor. Three men confessed, one of them a former county sheriff who testified that their object had simply been to run Morgan out of the United States into Canada. All denied any knowledge of what had happened to him subsequently. Since there was no corpse, and no evidence of murder, the convicted men were simply sentenced to short terms in prison.

The trial outcome provoked a new wave of anti-Masonic hysteria. Thousands of frightened Masons quit their lodges. In New York State alone six hundred lodges shrank to fifty in the space of a few years. Some defectors sought to appease the extremists by posing as redeemed sinners. After breaking with the Masons of Saratoga, the Reverend Lebbeus Armstrong assured his congregation, "I am convinced that the whole system of Masonry belongs to the power of darkness . . . that its tendency is to subvert the moral government of God!"

In vain did the Masons attempt to explain that their aims were simply religious toleration and charitable activities, or point out that great Masons like Washington and Franklin would scarcely have belonged to an ugly, terroristic conspiracy.

A New York Senate investigating committee report of 1829 equated the Masons with the early Jesuits who had "subjugated, without force of arms, one-half of the continent of America as the dominion of the Pope. This order has been crushed, but within the last 120 years another has arisen—the Society of Free and Accepted Masons . . . similar to the order of Jesuits and commanding a secrecy still more profound." The order of Oddfellows was also suspect as "disguised Masonry."

A National Anti-Masonic Convention gathered at Baltimore in September 1831. All "secret and affiliated societies" were denounced as "dangerous to the liberties and subversive to the laws of the country." Anti-Masonic newspapers and magazines flourished throughout the Northeast. A typical feature offered the confession of former New York Mayor Cadwallader D. Colden, who knew how to swim with the new political tide. He had been a Mason at twenty-one, he admitted, but then had grown to see "the vanity and folly and the evil tendency of Masonry."

The *Anti-Masonic Enquirer* of Rochester, New York, was edited by a shrewd and ambitious politician named Thurlow Weed. Largely through his efforts, the extremists were united into an Anti-Masonic Party that almost elected its candidate for Governor in 1831. The following year the party had grown strong enough to nominate its own candidate for President, and to introduce a bill in the Pennsylvania Legislature to strip Masons of the right to vote, hold office, or serve on juries.

Pennsylvania legislators reacted with outrage. "Anti-Masonry comes from the land of notions," said a committee report on the bill. "It envies the possessors of office. It is ignorant. It absurdly denounces, as a mysterious institution full of guilt and blood, a society of which your committee suppose ten or fifteen thousand of our most useful, intelligent and eminent citizens of all parties are members."

By 1834 anti-Masonic extremism had run its course. Thurlow Weed quickly led his followers into a coalition with the Whig (later the Republican) Party. Anti-Masons dissolved into Whigs as Weed engineered the election of William H. Seward as governor of New York in 1838; then of William Henry Harrison as President in 1840. Weed was one of the early breed of American opportunists skilled at manipulating extremist hatreds into ladders for their own unscrupulous careers.

A century later two European dictators were also to find the Masonic order a useful scapegoat for their ambitions. In 1922, Italy's Benito Mussolini outlawed Masonic organizations as "secret plotters against the state," and in 1933, Germany's Adolph Hitler followed suit. But despite a recurrent history of persecution in periods of extremism at home and abroad, the Masonic order has survived and thrived. Today in America there are over eleven thousand Masonic lodges and almost two million members.

At about the same time as the anti-Masonic madness, another wave of extremist intolerance swept through America—anti-Catholicism. Even before that, it had never been easy for Catholics in largely Protestant America. Prejudice had almost driven Charles Carroll, father of the signer of the Declaration of Independence, to leave colonial Maryland for French Louisiana. In 1774, a New England pamphlet objected bitterly when the Crown's Quebec Act recognized Catholic rights in Canada. "If Gallic Papists have a right to worship in their own way," it warned, "then farewell to the liberties of poor America!"

The 1830s brought a 400 percent jump in immigration, most of it from Catholic countries. Native-born Americans grew hostile as new Catholic churches, schools, and convents began to spring up in their midst. American workers resented the extra competition for jobs. Catholic immigrants were attacked on the streets of Boston by mobs, and their homes were stoned.

In 1830 an anti-Catholic newspaper appeared, reprinting lurid propaganda tracts imported from abroad with such titles as *Forty Popish Frauds Detected and Disclosed.* A year later a New York Protestant Association was formed to fight Catholicism. The Reverend Dr. Lyman Beecher, father of Harriet Beecher Stowe, orated loudly against "the Devil and the Pope of Rome."

A fanatical anti-Catholic explosion was ignited in 1834 when Elizabeth Harrison, a music teacher known as Sister Mary John, suffered a breakdown from overwork while teaching music at the Ursuline Convent boarding school in Charlestown, Massachusetts. Fleeing to the home of one of her pupils, she asked to be taken to a friend's home in West Cambridge. Here she quickly recovered, returned to the convent, and apologized for the disturbance she had caused by her flight.

But by this time a wild story was sweeping through Boston, fancifully embroidered and garbled with each retelling. As it reached a reporter's ears, Sister Mary was a nun who had incurred the displeasure of her tyrannical Mother Superior, and had been imprisoned in a convent dungeon. She had managed to escape, only to be captured and dragged back to the underground cells, which were overflowing with nuns and children imprisoned for penance. The *Boston Mercantile Journal* headlined the story "MYSTERIOUS."

Posters suddenly appeared all over Charlestown: TO THE SELECTMEN OF CHARLESTOWN! GENTLEMEN. . . . IT IS YOUR DUTY TO HAVE THIS AFFAIR INVESTIGATED IMMEDIATELY; IF NOT, THE TRUCKMEN OF BOSTON WILL DEMOLISH THE NUNNERY THURSDAY NIGHT!

A committee of five selectmen hastily called at the Ursuline Convent, to the indignation of the Mother Superior, Mother St. George. But Sister Mary John assured the visitors that she was not being held a captive, and also showed them through the empty basement of the convent. The selectmen reported publicly that the rumors were baseless, but anti-Catholic extremists had already fanned mob hysteria to fever pitch.

There was an eager willingness to believe the worst. A lurid book called *Six Months In a Convent* had recently appeared, purporting to be the confessions of an "escaped nun," Rebecca Reed. She told of being forced to take holy orders, undergoing cruel and unusual penances, and being held with other nuns in underground vaults as white slaves for priests.

New posters blossomed all over Boston and Charlestown: TO ARMS!! TO ARMS!! YE BRAVE AND FREE, THE AVENGING SWORD UNSHIELD!! LEAVE NOT ONE STONE UPON ANOTHER OF THAT CURST NUNNERY THAT PROSTITUTES FEMALE VIRTUE AND

THE KIDNAPPER.—A CASE FOR THE POLICE.

Kidnapper: "There's a beautiful veil!!! Give me your parcel, my dear, while you put it on."

This anti-Catholic cartoon implies that the Church was far more interested in money than in piety.

LIBERTY UNDER GARB OF HOLY RELIGION. WHEN BONAPARTE OPENED THE NUNNERIES IN EUROPE HE FOUND CORDS OF INFANT SKULLS!!!!!

At nine o'clock on the night of August 11, 1834, a howling mob of four thousand descended on the Ursuline Convent. Children asleep in the dormitory were awakened by the uproar.

"Down with the convent! Release your prisoners! Free the hidden nun!" Mob leaders pounded on the door, demanding admittance. Children began screaming. Nuns rushing to soothe them were frightened themselves. An outraged Mother St. George confronted the mob defiantly on the convent steps.

"Disperse immediately!" she cried out. "For if you don't, the Bishop has twenty thousand Irishmen at his command in Boston, and they will whip you all into the sea!" A hail of stones forced her to retreat and bar the door.

Rioters lit torches from a pile of tar barrels and set a fire on the grounds. A hogshead of rum was broached to fortify the brave warriors for the assault ahead. At midnight they flung rocks through the windows and tried to force the heavy door. When Mother St. George tried to talk to them again from a window, two muskets opened fire at her. She retreated hastily to the children's dormitory, where children and nuns were in a state of utter terror. Some children had fainted.

She led them in a hasty exodus from the convent through a back entrance, just as the mob burst into the building through smashed windows. The rioters raced from attic to cellars in a fruitless, drunken search for imprisoned nuns in dungeons. Consoling themselves by looting silverware and other valuables, they tossed Bibles, crucifixes, schoolbooks, and bedding into a heap on the first floor and started a bonfire. Some crusaders dashed through the convent setting the drapes afire.

The spectacular blaze brought fire companies from Charlestown, Boston, and Cambridge. No attempt was made to put out the conflagration, however, because the mob would not allow it. At dawn the fire was over and the rum cask empty. The crusaders returned home cheering and singing. Three convent pupils died from the effects of that night of wild terror and exposure.

The extremists were not yet finished. The following night they returned to destroy fences, trees, and anything still standing on the convent site. The next day there was a rumor that Bishop Fenwick had called upon Boston's Irish laborers to avenge the outrage. That night a thousand rioters with knives and pistols formed defiantly in front of the Catholic Church in Charlestown's Franklin Street. But no Irish appeared.

Bishop Fenwick had actually begged them not to answer violence with violence, but to trust to American justice.

A Protestant reaction against the extremists was not long in coming. Mass meetings in Charlestown and Boston denounced the mob's action and demanded the punishment of its ringleaders. But when four of the rioters were arrested and tried at Concord, all were acquitted but one adolescent, and he was pardoned. To make matters worse, in another arson case heard about the same time, two Boston men were convicted and hanged.

Two years later anti-Catholic prejudice was still so virulent that another lurid book "exposing" convents quickly became a runaway bestseller. *The Awful Disclosures of Maria Monk* professed to be the confession of a Protestant convert who had entered the Hotel Dieu Convent in Montreal. She first turned up in New York City, pregnant and blaming a priest. In her book, the convent from which she claimed to have escaped was characterized by the usual underground passageways, prison cells, brutal penances, forced embraces by priests, and baby murders.

"At least eighteen or twenty infants," she wrote, "were smothered and secretly buried in the cellar while I was a nun."

A public outcry of horror brought permission for a team of investigators led by New York City editor William L. Stone, a self-acknowledged anti-Catholic, to inspect the Hotel Dieu Convent. They found that Maria Monk had never been a nun there; that most of the nuns were past childbearing age; that there were no secret trapdoors or passageways; that Maria had been treated for emotional disorders; that her descriptions of the convent were wholly inaccurate; and that her book had been ghost written for her by a Reverend J. J. Slocum.

"MARIA MONK IS AN OUT AND OUT IMPOSTER," Stone reported in his New York *Commercial Advertiser,* "AND HER BOOK IN ALL ITS ESSENTIAL FEATURES A TISSUE OF CALUMNIES. . . . As a man of honor and professor of the Protestant faith, I MOST SOLEMNLY BELIEVE THAT THE PRIESTS AND NUNS ARE INNOCENT IN THIS MATTER."

The anti-Catholic extremists refused to give up. When Maria disappeared from New York in 1837, they quickly spread a new horror story about her abduction by six priests to the Catholic Asylum in Philadelphia. Dr. W. W. Sleigh, a leading Protestant physician of that city, investigated. He reported that the rumor was "a mass of falsehoods." Maria had left New York by herself, and "is at present incapable of taking care of herself." A dozen years later, forgotten and distraught, she died, a charity patient on New York's Welfare Island.

The wave of anti-Catholic extremism Maria Monk had revived persisted. It was kept alive by the stubborn intolerance of prominent Protestants like Samuel F. B. Morse, the inventor of the telegraph. In a book called *Foreign Conspiracy Against the Liberties of the United States,* he accused the Vatican of sending "Jesuit agents" to America to organize a plot for winning Catholic control of the United States by outvoting Protestants. He pointed out that Irish immigrants "clanned together, and kept alive their foreign feelings, associations, habits and manners." In his fanaticism he did not add that so did every non-Catholic immigrant group which felt insecure in America.

Morse called upon Protestants to form an "Anti-Popery Union." His prejudice infected millions of Americans who believed naively that a scientific genius who had been proved right about his telegraphy theory must also be right about Catholics. A Protestant Reformation Society organized in the late 1830s inspired persistent attacks upon the Pope and "Romanism."

This hate wave was intensified when the Irish potato famine brought an upsurge of immigration during the 1840s and 1850s. Many of the German newcomers who joined them were also Catholic. In 1843 the Protestant Reformation Society, alarmed by the political implications, organized an anti-Catholic, anti-alien party—the American Republicans. They depended upon Protestant prejudice and labor opposition to immigrants, who were accepting lower wages than American workers—only fifty cents a day—in the 1837–40 depression.

Trouble boiled over in the City of Brotherly Love when the Philadelphia School Board exempted Catholic pupils from religious exercises. "The Pope reigns in Philadelphia!" cried the American Republicans. When they held meetings and tried to vote in heavily Catholic districts, they were driven off by angry Irish Americans. In May 1844, they returned as a vengeful mob, burning down two Catholic churches and thirty homes, and fighting the state militia that had been called out to restore order.

Casualties of 30 killed and 150 wounded provoked a dismayed thunder of denunciation against "churchburners" from law-abiding Protestants. Both the Protestant Reformation Society and the American Republican Party were forced underground.

Their place was taken by the Native American Association, which insisted that European immigrants were too accustomed to tyranny to qualify as citizens of a democracy in only five years. The Native Americans demanded a twenty-one-year residence requirement before aliens could be naturalized and vote.

They also pressured Congress to drive immigrant poor off city welfare rolls, pointing out that some European governments actually paid their passage to America to rid their own taxpayers of the burden. The party grew influential enough to elect several Congressmen and Mayor James Harper in New York City.

Irish Catholic immigrants, who by 1855 made up 34 percent of New York City's voters, took determined political action to protect themselves from extremist Whigs, American Republicans, and Native Americans. They aligned themselves with the Democrats, who helped them out of trouble and got them city jobs. The "Irish cop on the beat" soon became a familiar figure in cities on the eastern seaboard—a development that did much to discourage anti-Catholic violence.

The Irish Catholic-Democratic coalition built strong political machines that captured many big cities of the Northeast. But not until 1928 did it feel strong enough to defy the extremists by running a Catholic for President.

6

Attacks on Privilege

Industrialists encouraged large-scale immigration to assure themselves of a plentiful supply of cheap labor. This allowed them to pay starvation wages to both foreign and native-born workers, who at the same time were charged high prices and outrageous rents for slum dwellings. Prices were kept high by industrialists who had monopolies in such necessities as matches, sugar, and fuel.

In 1829 angry labor extremists in New York City formed the Workingmen's Party, an early version of the Communist Party. Holding their first convention at Military Hall, they passed a series of resolutions that sent a thrill of fright through the power structure. "Hereditary transmission of wealth on the one hand and poverty on the other" were denounced as twin evils.

They called for an end to all privileges and monopolies, castigating bankers as "the greatest knaves, imposters . . . of the age." They demanded identical education for children of the poor and the rich, up to and through college—"as in a real republic, it should be." And they called upon all American workers to join their challenge to the Establishment.

At first professional politicians scoffed at the Working men's Party as a bad joke. But when the labor extremists put on a vigorous city election campaign that polled six thousand New York votes—out of a qualified twenty thousand—they were quickly taken seriously. The United States Bank, through its mouthpiece, the New York *Courier and Enquirer,* assailed them as immoral infidels whose doctrines threatened to topple the very foundations of private property and the American Republic.

The New York State Legislature took a more adroit tack. Introducing a few "reform" bills that paid lip service to the Party's objectives, but actually changed little, legislative leaders seduced the flattered Party firebrands into easing their pressure on the power structure. By 1831 the revolutionary movement was becalmed with no more wind in its sails.

Another oppressed minority of the period, Southern blacks, found it far more difficult to mount any kind of protest. Some slaves had masters who were paternalistic, out of either sentiment or a desire to keep a valuable property contented and working well in the cotton fields. But many slaves, treated little better than animals, lived lives of quiet desperation.

Yet even before the Revolution there were black extremists who rose against cruel masters, or against the institution of slavery. In 1741 a dozen New York City slaves rebelled against their masters and attempted to set the city ablaze. An even more extremist power structure sentenced them to be burned alive. The ringleader was "to be burned with a slow fire that he may continue in torment for eight or ten hours, and continue burning in the said fire until he be dead or consumed to ashes."

A slave insurrection broke out in Virginia in 1800, provoking Thomas Jefferson to prophesy gloomily, "We are truly to be pitied. . . . I tremble for my country when I reflect that God is just." He sought to trouble the conscience of his fellow countrymen by reminding them, "One *day* of American slavery is worse than a *thousand years* of what we rose in arms to oppose!"

Slavery was abolished by Argentina in 1813; Central America, in 1824, and Mexico, in 1829, but in the highly civilized

United States of 1832 slaves were valuable property bringing $500 apiece at auction. They were an excellent investment for plantation owners because slave labor cost as little as fifteen dollars a year. One pious lady planter of great wealth in central Mississippi worked her slaves from 3:30 a.m. until 9:00 p.m. every weekday, with her overseers using whips to keep them in line. On Sundays she preached the gospel to them.

Most Southern slave-owners rejected Thomas Jefferson's radical notions that slavery was not God-ordained and that slaves were not happy in servitude. "Several millions of human beings of an inferior race," Jefferson Davis once said, "are peaceful and contented laborers in their sphere."

The stereotype of banjo-strumming, carefree "darkies" was exploded in 1831 by a Virginia black extremist named Nat Turner. A religious fanatic, he was a slave owned by a Southampton County plantation owner named Joseph Travis, a kind master by Turner's own admission. "He placed the greatest confidence in me," Nat later revealed to journalist Thomas R. Gray. "In fact, I had no cause to complain of his treatment."

Turner, Gray reported, "was not instigated by motives of revenge or sudden anger, but the result of long deliberation and a settled purpose of mind—the offspring of gloomy fanaticism." He had decided that slavery was an evil institution, and that God had selected him to overturn it.

Turner declared he had seen a vision: "I saw white spirits and black spirits engaged in battle, and the sun was darkened; the thunder rolled in the heavens, and the blood flowed in streams." He heard a voice he took for the Holy Ghost telling him he had been called to pick up the yoke of Christ—"that I should take it on and fight against the Serpent, for the time was fast approaching when the first should be the last, and the last should be the first."

On February 12, 1831, an eclipse seemed to him a heavenly "sign" to begin planning his uprising. Soon sixty-six other slaves were sworn to revolt when he gave the signal. The rebellion began on Saturday, August 13, when Nat and six aides began breaking into the homes of Southampton County whites.

Beginning with the home of Turner's own master, they hacked fifty-seven white men, women, and children to death savagely with hatchet broadaxes. The only family spared was one of poor whites who owned no slaves. The blood bath went on for forty-eight terrible hours as terrified white families fled, some out of the county, others to hide in the woods or barricade themselves in public buildings. The news flashed through the South.

"The slaves are plotting! The Negroes have risen!"

Panicky Southerners were convinced that the Nat Turner uprising was the beginning of a full-scale black revolution. Troops from Fort Monroe, reinforced by artillery and sailors from two warships, sped to Southampton County. Between forty and a hundred blacks were shot down in cold blood. "All died bravely," said Governor Floyd of Virginia, "indicating no reluctance to lose their lives in such a cause." With nineteen others, Turner was captured, tried, and sentenced to hang.

Visiting the doomed rebel, reporter Gray wrote, "He is a complete fanatic . . . I looked on him, and my blood curdled in my veins." Nat Turner was swung into the air in the Virginia town of Jerusalem, a curiously appropriate place to die for a religious fanatic who believed the Lord had appointed him to kill.

His revolt sent shivers up and down the spines of all Southerners. "It is like a smothered volcano," declared Mrs. Lawrence Lewis, George Washington's niece. "We know not when, or where, the flame will burst forth, but we know that death in the most repulsive forms awaits us." She wrote to Boston begging its mayor, Harrison Gray Otis, to suppress the new abolitionist newspaper edited by William Lloyd Garrison, *The Liberator*, before it fell into the hands of Southern blacks and inflamed them into following Nat Turner's example.

Otis replied that he had no such power of suppression, and would not use it if he had. "Such violation of freedom of the press," he explained, "would only drive moderates to make common cause with the fanatics."

But Southern extremists had good reason to fear Northern extremists. The abolitionists were out to emancipate the slaves any way they could—by law or by breaking the law. In 1840 they organized the Liberty Party, with James G. Birney of New York as their Presidential nominee. The driving spirit behind the party was William Lloyd Garrison. At thirty-five, he was already a veteran of a decade of fighting slavery through *The Liberator*.

"I am in earnest," he had written in the first issue of January 1, 1831. "I will not equivocate—I will not excuse—I will not retreat an inch—AND I WILL BE HEARD!"

The paper had grown quickly in influence, if not in funds. Garrison was so poor that he often had to sleep on the floor of his print shop. When the State of Georgia offered a five thousand dollar reward for his arrest and conviction, he laughed wryly, "I am tempted to claim it myself!"

He was enraged by a system of American "justice" which his friend, escaped slave Frederick Douglass, described in these terms: "To be accused was to be convicted, and to be convicted was to be punished." Garrison wrote grimly, "Let Southern oppressors tremble; let their secret abettors tremble; let their Northern apologists tremble; let all the enemies of the persecuted blacks tremble. . . . Cost what it may, every slave on the American soil must be liberated from his chains."

Otherwise, he insisted, North must split from South.

He was under no illusions about the price abolitionists would have to pay for their extremism. Death threats were made to him daily. "What I have to offer you," he told his followers in *The Liberator*, "is fatigue, danger, struggle, death." On October

21, 1835, a Boston mob of abolition-haters seized him from a speaker's platform, put a rope around his neck and dragged him through the streets until police rescued him.

Mob violence against the abolitionists grew steadily. Three times the presses of the Reverend Elijah Lovejoy were smashed by pro-slavery extremists. Editing the Alton, Illinois *Observer* in 1837, he tried to defend his presses from being wrecked a fourth time. The enraged mob murdered him. Such savagery sickened Americans and drove 150,000 into the abolitionist camp, among them such celebrated names as John Greenleaf Whittier, Henry Wadsworth Longfellow, and James Russell Lowell.

Abolitionists were divided into militants and supporters. It was the extremists who organized the illegal Underground Railroad, an ingenious network of "depots," or friendly homes, along a flight route to Canada. Runaway slaves would be guided from one depot to another by "conductors" until they reached safety. Some escaped slaves returned to serve as guides for others. Harriet Tubman, an illiterate field hand, risked her life persistently to help free over three hundred other slaves.

The South reacted violently. Brutal slave hunters were offered bounties for pursuing black runaways and bringing them back in irons. Abolitionists suspected of being in the Underground Railroad were threatened with violence, house-burning, and murder. The slave catchers often kidnapped free Northern blacks in place of slaves they could not catch, leading to wild clashes with infuriated abolitionists.

Southern Congressmen forced passage of the Fugitive Slave Act of 1850, compelling federal aid in apprehending runaways, and providing fines and jail for anyone attempting to interfere. Extremism on both sides flared to new heights.

Revolt against a different sort of enslavement took place in New York State. The "anti-rent war," sometimes called the "Tinhorn

Rebellion," was a unique extremist movement, yet one of the least-known, in American history.

The Hudson River Valley region was owned lock, stock, and barrel by a handful of patroons, or manor lords—Schuylers, Livingstons, Van Rensselaers, Van Cortlandts—who continued to rule the area as though it were still 1629 and the Dutch West India Company still made them all-powerful.

By 1838 something like a hundred thousand tenant farmers lived on lands owned by the Van Rensselaers alone. The renters were bound by a "lease" that compelled them to pay all kinds of feudal dues and taxes as rent—in effect mortgage payments, but without ever gaining title to lands, farms, or homes. Alexander Hamilton, whose wife had been a Schuyler, had drawn up the "model" contract which tenants had been forced to sign ever since.

In 1838 the patroons' discontented serfs, grandsons of the original tenants, staged anti-rent riots on the Rensselaer estate in Albany County. They were promptly jailed. Some were friends and cousins of Dr. Smith Boughton, a tall, slender young physician with a deceptively quiet manner and distinguished white hair. Determined to fight patroon injustice, he consulted immigrant agitator Thomas Devyr, who had had experience fighting tyrannical landlords in Ireland.

With Devyr's help, Boughton drew up a "Statement of Grievances and Proposed Redress," demanding a constitutional amendment to end the feudal leasehold system that enslaved the Hudson River Valley farmers. It was quickly signed by several thousand manor farmers, and Boughton took it to Albany to ask for appropriate legislation. Nervous assemblymen dropped the hot potato in the laps of a judiciary committee.

The committee stalled by insisting that Boughton produce legal support for his proposed amendment. So he went to Boston where Daniel Webster gave it his endorsement, growling,

THE ANTI-RENT RIOT.

Culver Pictures, Inc.
The Anti-Rent Riot was a protest by New York State land tenants against onerous rent conditions.

"If I had the time, I would tear that manor apart!" But when Boughton returned to Albany, he found a frigid reception that made it clear that agents of the Van Rensselaers had been consulted, and had paid enough to deafen committee ears.

Boughton returned home angrily determined that if justice was not to be had through legal methods, then he would seize it for the farmers by extremist tactics. A secret order of tenants was organized calling themselves "the Indians," evoking memories of the "Indians" of Sam Adams's Boston Tea Party. They concealed their identities by wearing weird masks and Indian-like costumes with bright tin horns hung from their belts. Armed with pitchforks, hatchets, homemade spears, clubs, pistols, and rifles, they marched in ranks to fife and drums.

They hailed their chief with the roar, "Big Thunder!"

Big Thunder cried back, "Down with the rent!"

The Indians blew their horns and waved their weapons.

Big Thunder inflamed them with an angry speech accusing the Livingstons and Van Rensselaers of having robbed them, their fathers and grandfathers, by rents that by now had paid many times over for the lands and homes they still did not own. "Do not pay the robber lords their rents," he urged. "When the sheriffs come to take your farms, the Indians will come to your rescue and drive them off. No one will know who we are, where we came from or where we went!"

The anti-rent war began. Sheriffs attempting to serve dispossess notices were met by masked men blowing tin horns. The cacaphony would swiftly bring a charging band of masked "Indians" in war regalia, and the sheriffs usually beat a hasty retreat. When one stood his ground, he was tarred and feathered. A group of masked farmers who attempted to halt the carriage of General Jacob Livingston fled when he drew two pistols and opened fire.

Big Thunder called a giant rally in Columbia County. Thousand of jubilant Hudson Valley "braves" put on a show of whooping, leaping, Indian dancing, blowing their horns and firing blanks into the air. Suddenly Bill Rifenburg, young son of one of the farmers, was accidentally killed by a gun firing real bullets instead of blanks. Shocked, Big Thunder called off the demonstration.

A little later he and other "Indian" leaders were deploring the incident at Barn's Tavern when Sheriff Henry Miller, who had previously been driven off while trying to serve dispossess notices, entered the taproom with four deputies.

"You're under arrest, Doctor Boughton," the sheriff told Big Thunder. A band of "Indians" rushed forward to try to fight off the officers, but Boughton was hustled off to jail in Hudson.

That night the valley echoed to the blasts of Indian horns. Thousands of torches lit up both sides of the river as they moved toward Hudson. Mayor Curtis was warned to release Boughton or watch his town burn to ashes. Alarmed, he rushed an appeal to Governor William H. Seward for troops, and they came with flags flying, drums beating, artillery pieces ready for action. The discouraged "Indians" melted away.

Soon afterward in Delaware County the "Indians" opened fire on a sheriff's posse attempting to dispossess a farmer, and a deputy was killed. Governor Silas Wright, Seward's successor, pushed a law through the New York Legislature punishing any man who carried arms while disguised. Declaring Delaware County to be in a "state of insurrection," he ordered sixty farmers arrested and jailed, two on charges of murder.

The valley patroons were determined to strike terror into the hearts of their rebel renters. The magistrate chosen for the Boughton trial, Judge John W. Edmunds, and the prosecutor, Attorney General John Van Buren, were their hand-picked choices, along with a stacked jury. Edmunds identified Boughton as Big Thunder, "the leader, the principal fomenter of all these disturbances." Although the formal charge had been reduced to only "robbery," in order to ensure conviction, Edmunds snapped, "The offense in fact is high treason, rebellion against your government, and armed insurrection." Then he sentenced Doctor Boughton to prison for the rest of his life.

This excessive injustice by the Hudson Valley power structure appalled not only New York State but the whole nation. Boughton refused to appeal, feeling it would be futile. He decided to accept his martyrdom and wait in jail for an aroused public wrath to crash down around the ears of the arrogant feudal barons. Five thousand leasehold farmers wept openly as he was led off in irons. Six of the Delaware County rioters were also sentenced to life terms.

Thomas Devyr, who had helped Boughton draw up the original renters' bill of protest, started an Albany weekly called *The Anti-Renter*. Persistently agitating for the release of Boughton and other victims of patroon injustice, he urged farmers to abandon militant revolt and fight the land barons instead at the ballot box. "Keep within the bounds of the law," he cautioned. "But be up and onward!"

Mounting an election campaign against "Patroon law and Landlord judges," they won enough popular support in 1846 to sweep Governor Silas Wright out of office. Their successful nominee, Democrat John Young, immediately issued a full pardon for Dr. Boughton and the other anti-rent prisoners.

Reforms in the state constitution provided for the popular election of judges, as well as abolishing "feudal tenures of every description" and making illegal any "lease or grant of agricultural land for a longer period than twelve years."

On advice of young lawyer Samuel J. Tilden, later Governor of New York, tenants brought suit against the Van Rensselaers and won legal title to their farms. In 1852 the Van Rensselaers, the Livingstons and the rest of the feudal barons threw in the sponge and gloomily resigned themselves to the end of an era.

Tenant lands began passing into the hands of the farmers who lived on and cultivated them.

Dr. Smith Boughton, the extremist who had begun the successful revolt and almost spent his entire life in jail for the cause, used his life instead to serve the region as a greatly esteemed and much-loved country doctor. When he retired at the age of seventy in 1880, most of his patients were his old fellow warriors of the Indian days or their sons—landowners all now, thanks to him.

"It is time not to mix any more in the turmoils and busy scenes of life," old Dr. Boughton smiled as he laid up his buggy whip. His work was done.

7

The Extremist World
of Horace Greeley

Not one but dozens of extremist movements swirled around the head of a giant crusader of the nineteenth century—Horace Greeley. A cantankerous, outspoken, idealistic country boy turned big city editor, Greeley made the New York *Tribune* the most controversial newspaper in America. "People buy it," a rival editor said in disgust, "to see what new outrageous things Greeley has found to shock them with."

He denounced the power structure for failing to provide work for the jobless, and for letting their children starve. A Boston judge who jailed an atheist for blasphemy was blistered as an idiot. The government was accused of murdering Indians. Greeley argued for labor unions and free homesteads; against capital punishment, military forces, and white bread.

He was a scornful foe of religious extremists like William Miller, who was convinced that the second coming of Christ and the end of the world would take place on October 22, 1843. Miller persuaded thousands of his Adventist followers to sell their homes and belongings, put on "holy ascension robes" which he sold them at a profit, and wait with him on roofs, hilltops, and haystacks for a quicker ascent to heaven.

Greeley's own extremism was reflected in his eccentric dress—a white duster, a low-crowned farmer's hat on the back of a huge head of white hair, drooping spectacles that gave him an owl-like appearance, a crumpled shirt, necktie askew, a leg of his shapeless trousers flopping over a mud-spattered country boot, stockings falling over his heels.

"He is a man who could save a Nation," an early admirer wrote, "but never learn to tie a cravat."

When he was twenty-nine, Greeley was chosen by Thurlow Weed to mastermind the Whig Party's election campaign of 1840. Their presidential candidate was William Henry Harrison, a former Indian fighter who had won the obscure Battle of Tippecanoe. To lure Southern votes, John Tyler of Virginia was nominated for Vice President. There were no real campaign issues and Weed wanted none. He instructed Greeley to whip up a circus enthusiasm for the Whigs, dramatizing the election as a choice between the foppish Democratic incumbent, Van Buren, and a "country boy" reared in an Ohio frontier log cabin.

Greeley's campaign was a masterpiece of irrelevance.

He drummed home a nonsensical slogan, "Tippecanoe and Tyler, too!" in emotional mass meetings, torchlight parades, fireworks, and campaign songs. ("What has caused this great commotion, motion, motion, Our country through? It is the ball a-rollin' on . . . for Tippecanoe and Tyler too!") The nation waved Tippecanoe flags, wore Tippecanoe badges, blew their noses in Tippecanoe handkerchiefs, washed with Tippecanoe soap. Every town had its log cabin, its Tippecanoe club and chorus.

A whispering campaign accused President Van Buren of spraying his whiskers with French *eau de cologne,* sleeping in a Louis XV bed, eating French food from silver plates, and riding in a British-made gilded coach. One Democratic journalist sneered that if old Tippecanoe were given two thousand dollars and a jug of hard cider, he'd be happier in a log cabin than in the White House. Greeley seized gleefully on this admission that the Whig candidate was a "simple man of the people." He flooded the country with log-cabin badges, songs, clubs, and even log cabins where thirsty voters could toast old Tippecanoe with hard cider while they read the Whig campaign paper, *Log Cabin*.

The Whigs won, making Thurlow Weed a power in the White House, and Horace Greeley so ashamed of himself that he vowed never again to be party to so extremist a scheme for bamboozling the American people. In fact, he broke with Weed and the Whig Party shortly after their victory.

One of the extremists championed enthusiastically by Greeley was Henry Thoreau, the writer-naturalist who preached that the way to defeat the law when it is tyrannical is to organize mass civil disobedience and fill the jails.

When the US declared war on Mexico on May 13, 1846, Thoreau—like Greeley and Abraham Lincoln—denounced the action as an imperialist adventure to expand slave territory. He resisted the only way he felt he could—by refusing to pay his Massachusetts poll tax. This example was followed a century later by folk singer Joan Baez, who refused to pay that portion of her income tax which would be spent by the government in armaments and prosecution of the Vietnam War.

"I was not born to be forced," Thoreau insisted. So he was flung into jail at Concord, Massachusetts. His friend and mentor, Ralph Waldo Emerson, hurried to the prison to ask in amazement, "What are you doing in there, Henry?" Fixing him with a sardonic glance, Thoreau replied, "What are you doing out there, Waldo?" Released when his aunt insisted upon paying his tax, Thoreau told the jailer angrily, "I'll be back again next year. I will *never* pay tax to any government for an unjust cause!" And he never did.

His essay on *Civil Disobedience* became a classic, urging mass civil disobedience to unjust laws, and going to jail if necessary, rather than outrage the conscience by obeying them. Thoreau's doctrine became the inspiration for Mahatma Gandhi's campaign to win independence for India, the Reverend Martin Luther King's campaign to win civil rights for black Americans, and the draft-defying campaign led by Dr. Benjamin Spock and Reverend William Sloane Coffin to protest the Vietnam War.

Thoreau's critics argued that violence might grow out of the mass demonstrations he advocated. "Suppose blood should flow," he replied. "Is there not a sort of blood shed when the conscience is wounded? Through this wound a man's real manhood and immortality flow out, and he bleeds to an everlasting death. I see this blood flowing now!"

An active abolitionist in the Underground Railroad, he supported extremist John Brown's raid on Harper's Ferry. Concord's selectmen refused to ring the Town Hall's bell to signal his speech on behalf of Brown, so Thoreau rang it himself. "When were the good and the brave," he cried to his audience, "ever in the majority? . . . Is it not possible that an individual may be right and a government wrong?"

One of Greeley's pet enthusiasms was the Utopian colony movement of the 1840s. Idealistic extremists, rebelling against the Establishment of the era, sought to found perfect new communities on the model envisioned in 1516 by Sir Thomas More in his *Utopia*. There would be no rich, no poor. All would work part-time on the land, part-time at a trade. All would wear the same clothes, eat prescribed health foods, share a cultural program, marry as directed by eugenic magistrates, and bring up their children by colony rules.

In 1840 Utopian extremists met in a Boston convention called the Friends of Universal Reform. Ralph Waldo Emerson described the gathering: "Madmen, mad-women, men with beards, Dunkers, Muggletonians, Groaners, Agrarians, Seventh-Day Baptists, Quakers, Abolitionists, Calvinists, Unitarians, and Philosophers—all came successively to the top, and seized their moment, if not their hour, wherein to chide, or pray, or protest." They included Bronson Alcott, father of Louisa May; Dr. William Ellery Channing, founder of Unitarianism; Thoreau; James Russell Lowell; and William Lloyd Garrison. Greeley was absent only because of the Tippecanoe campaign.

Extremists they all were, but driven by a common compulsion to find a practical way to apply Christian principles to the American way of life. Like many restless, dissatisfied Americans of the late 1960s, they felt that moral meaning and intellectual values were missing from a prospering society that had grown too materialistic.

Experimental colonies began to appear in the northeast, like the Brook Farm Phalanx at West Roxbury, a Boston suburb. Made up largely of intellectuals, the men dressed as farmers in peasant blouses, the women in muslin or calico. Labors were divided among the Cattle Group, the Milking Group, the Plowing Group, the Nursery Group, and the Culinary Group. Emerson described Brook Farm, which had seventy to eighty members, as "a perpetual picnic, a French Revolution." It lasted three years until a fire and financial troubles caused its demise.

The Fruitlands Community of Harvard town was founded by Bronson Alcott with strict vegetarians who also shunned slave-grown fish, butter, eggs, milk, cheese, coffee, tea, and molasses. They ate only their own homegrown "aspiring" vegetables—those that grew upward—as they were against root vegetables that "burrow into the earth." Fruitlands males proved less interested in weeding than in making "philosophical visits" to other Utopian colonies. Women and children were left behind to harvest the crops. Fruitlands lasted six months.

A colony called Modern Times was founded on Long Island by America's first anarchist, Josiah Warren, known as "the Peaceful Revolutionist." Each colonist was free to do—or not do—as he pleased. Everything was sold at cost, plus a fee for the seller's time. Marriage was forbidden; any other arrangements were a matter of taste. Warren spent most of his time playing the French horn. The colony quickly fell apart under an influx of drifters who today might be classified as beatniks or hippies.

Greeley himself fell under the spell of Albert Brisbane, an enthusiastic disciple of a French Utopian named Fourier. Fourierism called for a Communist society of four to five hundred families living in a commune, owning and cultivating the land together. All shared food, shelter, and clothing—garbage collectors on equal terms with teachers. Fourierism promised an end to poverty, misery, and crime.

Greeley helped launch the Sylvania Phalanx in Pike County, Pennsylvania, donating a year's profits from the *Tribune,* five thousand dollars, to found it. "When I took up this cause," he told the first Fourierist Convention in April 1844, "I knew that I went in the teeth of many of my patrons, in the teeth of the prejudices of the great mass, in the teeth of religious prejudices. I confess I had a great many more clergymen on my subscription list before than I have now."

But the Sylvania Phalanx was a dismal failure. Adults quarreled. Children ran wild. The land was stony and untillable. Intellectuals preferred to think than work. The experiment died after eighteen months. Disillusioned, Greeley lost his faith in the perfectability of human nature.

Two Utopian societies did succeed. One was the Shaker community; Greeley felt that it had been saved because of its foundation upon a strong religious bond. The other was the Oneida Community of "Perfectionists" founded in upstate New York by

John Humphrey Noyes, a radical who had been driven out of Vermont. Oneida flourished for thirty years.

The Perfectionists initiated many extremist ideas about human relationships. Love affairs were allowed as long as no children resulted. Parenthood required eugenic marriages approved by a committee of elders. Only couples above average physically and mentally were permitted to have children.

Oneida finances were assured by the sale of two colony handicrafts—steel traps invented by a Perfectionist, and plated silverware of great beauty. Legal attacks against the colony's extremist moral standards, however, forced its dissolution in 1880. Oneida Community, Limited, survived as a stock company continuing to produce fine silverware.

Greeley was one of the early champions of the feminists who launched a women's rights movement against the patriarchal power structure. They began by attacking the Fourteenth Amendment, which limited the right to vote to "male citizens." But they were soon fighting for equal rights with men in everything—to drink, smoke, have love affairs, wear pants, become doctors. "Let them be sea captains if they will!" cried Margaret Fuller.

If all feminists seemed extremists to most men of the period, only a small number were shockingly radical. They were often shunned by leaders of the women's rights movement, like Victoria Claflin Woodhull, who preferred free love to marriage. With Cornelius Vanderbilt's help she became the first woman broker on Wall Street. She published a weekly advocating herself as the first Lady President. She crusaded for short skirts, birth control, free love, vegetarianism, a ban on capital punishment, world government, and easy divorce laws.

The first full English version of the *Communist Manifesto* appeared in her paper. She was arrested for publishing charges of immorality and hypocrisy against the Reverend Henry Ward

"WOMAN'S KINGDOM IS AT HOME"

Culver Pictures, Inc.
The women's rights movement created a great furor both for and against the feminists.

Beecher, the nation's most prominent clergyman. While in jail she ran for President on an Equal Rights ticket with abolitionist leader Frederick Douglass as her Vice Presidential candidate. She actually took several thousand votes away from Ulysses S. Grant.

One of the earliest feminist extremists was a Scotswoman immigrant, Frances Wright, who in 1824 founded the Utopian colony of Nashoba in western Tennessee. Buying the freedom of slaves, she brought them to Nashoba for schooling. Also scorning marriage as the "robbery and murder" of women, she had open love affairs that scandalized Tennesseans, who forced Nashoba to shut down. She resettled the freed slaves in Haiti, then joined philanthropist Robert Dale Owen in a new Socialist Utopia at New Harmony, Pennsylvania. But even their combined resources were too thin for "a thousand eaters and few workers."

The first Women's Rights Convention was called in Seneca Falls, New York, on July 19, 1848. One leading spirit was Elizabeth Cady Stanton, who spent her honeymoon in London attending the 1840 World Anti-Slavery Convention. Another was a Quaker, Lucretia Mott, the first American woman to address a masculine gathering. A courageous crusader, she invaded slave territory and openly preached abolition to infuriated mobs.

Abolitionist Lucy Stone created a sensation when she married Henry Blackwell and had him sign a marriage contract, called a "Protest," in which he agreed to let her retain her maiden name in marriage. Blackwell's sister Elizabeth outraged America's doctors by becoming the first lady MD in 1849, going on to found the New York Infirmary and College for Women.

Dr. Mary Walker went into the Civil War as a commissioned assistant surgeon, wearing pants and a long flapping coat. After her war service, for which she received a bronze medal, she lectured in striped trousers, frock coat and silk hat, campaigning against the nicotine evil." She carried a rolled umbrella with which she would often coldly knock cigars out of the mouths of astonished male smokers.

Bethenia Owens, the first woman doctor in the Far West, outraged local male physicians by daring to perform a public autopsy on a male corpse. "May I ask you to explain the difference," she challenged them, "between the attendance of a woman physician at a male autopsy, and the attendance of a man physician at a female autopsy?" But the indignant citizenry threatened her with tar and feathers, driving her out of Roseburg, Oregon, to seek a more broadminded community.

Few suffragettes were considered more extremist than Amelia Jenks Bloomer, who in 1851 dared appear on the street in full Turkish trousers. Creating a sensation, she persuaded other suffragettes to join her revolt against a society that imprisoned women in cumbersome petticoats and hoopskirts. But women reformers who dared wear her "Bloomers" were jeered and mocked by men and boys, who paid far more attention to what the "Bloomer Girls" wore than what they preached.

"If the women mean to wear the pants," editor James Gordon Bennett wrote sarcastically in his New York *Herald,* "then they must also be ready in case of war to buckle on the sword!" The suffragettes endured taunting for two years, then gave up the "reform dress" and retreated to hoopskirts.

Dorothea Dix, a spinster schoolteacher of New England, carried on a unique crusade of her own—to end the cruel and barbarous treatment of the mentally ill. Investigating the dungeons of institutions for four years, she traveled over ten thousand miles by stagecoach, steamboat, and horseback. She inspected and demanded reforms in eighteen prisons, three hundred jails, over five hundred almshouses and other institutions where the mentally ill were often kept naked in chains, starved, frozen, and whipped into obedience.

Her stagecoach was once held up by bandits. When Dorothea scolded them tartly, one of the robbers exclaimed, "My God, I know that voice! You're Dorothea Dix—I heard you speak in the Walnut Street jail in Philadelphia. God bless you, ma'am!" He forthwith ordered the robbers to return all the passengers' watches, jewelry, and money.

She forced one state legislature after another to build hospitals and asylums to give the mentally ill humane treatment. Wardens, town councils, and state officials bitterly attacked her as an interfering old crackpot. But singlehanded, crusading doggedly for over forty years, extremist Dorothea Dix ended America's medieval persecution of the mentally ill.

In some respects the idealistic extremist movements of the 1840s and 1850s were a disgusted reaction to Establishment extremism. The power structure was determined upon a course of American expansion by aggressive annexation. In just thirty-five months between 1845 and 1848, the United States added to its adjacent territory one out of every three square miles we occupy today, stretching from the western boundaries of the Louisiana Purchase to the Pacific. Annexation was accomplished under the justification that it was America's "Manifest Destiny" to expand its borders.

This expression, which became the rallying cry of jingo extremists, was first used by John L. O'Sullivan, editor of the *Democratic Review,* in July 1845. He referred to "our manifest destiny to overspread the continent allotted by Providence for the free development of our yearly multiplying millions." It did not disturb him in the least that different flags flew over adjacent lands. "Away, away with all those cobweb tissues of rights of discovery, exploration, settlement. . . . The Great Engineer of the Universe has fixed the natural limits of our country. . . . To that boundary we shall go, peacefully if we can, forcibly if we must."

Manifest Destiny extremism became the policy of the Democratic Party. Millions of Americans were persuaded not only that it was an "inevitable" pattern of growth for the United States, but that they had a God-given duty to bring the blessings of God-given American Protestantism to "savage or senile peoples." The New York *Herald* referred to Indians and Mexicans as "reptiles" who must "either crawl or be crushed."

William Henry Harrison, before his election as President, demanded, "Is one of the fairer portions of the globe to remain in a state of nature, the haunt of a few wretched savages, when it seems destined by the Creator to give support to a large population and to be the seat of civilization, of science, and of true religion?"

At the New Jersey Democratic Convention in 1844, delegates were brought to their feet cheering frantically a speaker who declared, "Make way . . . for the young American Buffalo—he has not yet got land enough. . . . The mighty Pacific and the turbulent Atlantic shall be his!" Four years later an "All Mexico" movement of Democrats demanded that the United States grab all of Mexico, Central America, and Cuba.

But to these Americans, extremists meant only objecters like Thoreau and Greeley, the Utopians, and the feminists.

8

Imperialists, Vigilantes, and Know-Nothings

Texas, which thirty thousand American settlers had broken away from Mexico in 1836, won noisy support from Manifest Destiny extremists for its application for admission to the Union. But a bitter nine-year fight ensued because the North wanted no more slave territory added to the South's strength. In 1844 the Democratic nominee, Manifest Destiny enthusiast James K. Polk, narrowly defeated Whig candidate Henry Clay for the White House.

Texas was swiftly annexed. Polk then set out to seize the Oregon territory, which today is Canadian British Columbia; part of Alberta; all of Oregon, Washington, and Idaho; and sections of Montana and Wyoming. His demands would have pushed the United States' northwest border up to the south of Alaska. His Manifest Destiny followers waved the flag, shouting, "Fifty-four forty or fight!" They demanded war unless England yielded all land south of that parallel of latitude. They neither knew nor cared that north of the Columbia River there were exactly eight American citizens.

Polk knew that his claim for this territory was feeble. Seeking for a gimmick to make it legal, he resuscitated a unilateral United States proclamation that had gathered dust for over two decades. He demanded that Britain withdraw from joint occupancy of the Oregon territory before "national honor and interest" compelled the United States to "enforce the Monroe Doctrine."

Manifest Destiny extremists were delighted. War with Britain would provide a pretext for taking over all of Canada. But the South was cool toward a war that would only add free soil territory to the North. So Polk quickly agreed to an English compromise proposal that simply extended the forty-ninth parallel, separating eastern United States from Canada, to the West Coast.

The focus of Manifest Destiny then switched to Mexico, which had broken off diplomatic relations with the United States following its annexation of Texas. Polk sent a special envoy, John Slidell, to offer the Mexicans 25 million dollars for California and the Southwest. When they refused to see him, Slidell told Polk indignantly, "Nothing is to be done with these people until they have been chastised!" Polk promptly sent General Zachary Taylor to invade disputed border territory and build a fort blockading the Rio Grande. When Mexicans tried to drive out Taylor's forces, Polk told Congress, "Mexico . . . has invaded our territory and shed American blood upon the American soil." He asked for and won a declaration of war on May 13, 1846.

Appalled by Polk's extremism, Whig Congressman Abraham Lincoln of Illinois branded the war as "unnecessarily and unconstitutionally begun by the President." He challenged Polk to name the spot on truly American soil where blood had been shed by any Mexican. Greeley's *Tribune* charged that Polk was betraying American ideals by sending young boys to murder Mexicans and be killed themselves. His angry editorial called "What Means This War?" declared, "It means that the Commandments are to be read and obeyed. . . . Thou *shalt* kill Mexicans. Thou *shalt* steal from them, hate them, burn their houses, ravage their fields, and fire red-hot cannon balls into towns swarming with their wives and children!"

Five days after war was declared, Polk sent Colonel Stephen W. Kearney to seize New Mexico and California. "We do not believe it possible," Greeley protested, "that our country *can* be prospered by such a war as this. These victories, these acquisitions, will prove immense calamities, by sapping the morals of our people, by inflating them with pride and the lust of conquest and of gold." He called Taylor's battles in Mexico "border ruffian aggressions . . . acts of a drama of naked villainy" intended to strengthen "the Slave Power."

Manifest Destiny extremists threatened to horsewhip him as an unpatriotic radical. "It is President Polk who is unpatriotic," he snapped. "I want American boys brought home where they belong, alive and uncrippled!" Protest against the Mexican War was so strong that one Whig paper in Boston printed an angry prayer that "the hordes under Taylor and [General] Scott be swept into the next world." Bitter Whigs in Congress proposed blocking any further war appropriations.

Alarmed by the division in the country, Polk dispatched a personal envoy, Nicholas P. Trist, Chief Clerk of the State Department, to force the Mexicans to accept harsh United States peace terms. But when Trist decided the terms were unrealistically extreme, Polk indignantly fired him. To Polk's astonishment Trist refused to be fired. With General Scott he managed to locate a moderate Mexican faction willing to sign a compromise—the Treaty of Guadalupe Hidalgo—and bring the war to a close.

Polk branded his defiant emissary "an impudent and unqualified scoundrel," but did not dare repudiate the treaty, which gave the United States extravagant enough spoils. The Mexicans ceded what is now California, Nevada, Utah and portions of Arizona, New Mexico, Colorado, and Wyoming. The Rio

Grande was established as the Texas border. Mexico received fifteen million dollars and immunity to three million dollars in claims by American citizens.

A Northern Whig damned it as "the treaty negotiated by an unauthorized agent, with an unacknowledged government, submitted by an accidental President, to a dissatisfied Senate."

Manifest Destiny extremists were delighted with the extension of American borders in the West and South, and pressed for expansion into the Caribbean. A secret society of Southerners called Knights of the Golden Circle worked feverishly to enlarge Southern territory as part of a plan to break away from the Union and form an independent slave republic.

When Polk obligingly tried to buy Cuba from Spain for a hundred million dollars, he was told, "We would prefer seeing it sunk in the ocean." So between 1849 and 1851 Manifest Destiny extremists mounted a military operation remarkably similar to the United States attempt in 1961 to seize Castro's Cuba, with the same ill-fated results as the Bay of Pigs disaster.

A Venezuelan expatriate, Narciso Lopez, led four hundred American "volunteers" on three unsuccessful military expeditions against Cuba from United States soil. The third invasion, landing near Havana, was captured by the Spanish. Lopez was strangled to death, fifty others were shot, and the rest sentenced to hard labor in Cuban mines. Swallowing hard, Secretary of State Daniel Webster apologized to Spain and paid a ransom for the convicted Americans, who were then freed and returned.

This blow to American pride led Democratic President Franklin K. Pierce to promise in his inaugural address of 1863 that he would annex "certain possessions not within our jurisdiction." His Secretary of State, William L. Marcy, sent Pierre Soule to Spain as the American minister with orders to buy Cuba for 130 million dollars or else "direct your efforts . . . to detach that island from Spain." Both efforts failed. Marcy promptly blamed

Soule for "exceeding his authority," deliberately concealing his own order to Soule to grab Cuba if necessary.

One Manifest Destiny adventurer, William Walker, persuaded multimillionaire Cornelius Vanderbilt to finance a scheme to conquer Central America for both commercial advantages and United States annexation. Vanderbilt was the extremist tycoon who had once said contemptuously, "What do I care about the law? Hain't I got the power?"

With a force of only fifty-seven mercenaries, Walker made himself dictator of revolution-torn Nicaragua. But when he tried to apply Manifest Destiny to the rest of Central America for the benefit of the Vanderbilt interests, he was captured in 1860 by the British and turned over to a Honduran firing squad for execution as an advance agent of American imperialism.

The jingoistic hysteria of Manifest Destiny subsided as Americans approached the Civil War era because the North opposed further additions of slave territory, and the South was equally determined to halt the spread of free soil.

The westward surge of America in the nineteenth century produced another form of extremism—the vigilante movement. Law and order were the last arrivals in Western towns and settlements. Often the first law officers appointed were either afraid of outlaws or were outlaws themselves. Vigilante committees—groups of outraged citizens of property and their employees—took the law into their own hands, pursuing and hanging suspected lawbreakers. They often made mistakes.

The discovery of gold in California in January 1848, brought adventure-seekers to San Francisco from all over the world. "Sydney Ducks"—escaped convicts and ticket-of-leave men, or probationers, from Australia's penal settlements—dominated an underworld district called Sydneytown, later known as the Barbary Coast. What few courts there were in the territory were hopelessly inadequate, like that of Judge Meade, who had two abominations—Mexicans and cigarette-smoking.

Once when a Mexican charged with stealing a horse was brought before him, Meade demanded, "Do you smoke cigarettes?"

"Si, *Senor Alcalde.*"

"Blow the smoke through your nose?"

"Si, *Senor Alcalde.*"

"Then I find you guilty as charged, and may God have mercy on your soul! Constable, take this fellow out and shoot him. He stole the horse sure enough!"

But criminals with the proper political connections could be sure of getting away with murder. In 1851 when one of the Sydney Ducks robbed and almost killed a storekeeper in San Francisco, a suspect was arrested. A crowd of five thousand grim San Franciscans rallied by prominent citizen Sam Brannan surrounded the court and demanded that the suspect be turned over to them.

"*We* are the Mayor and the recorder, the hangman and the laws," Brannan yelled. "I want no technicalities. Such things are devised to shield the guilty!" But police fought off the mob and tried the victim, who had no political pull. He was sentenced to fourteen years' imprisonment. He later proved to be innocent.

Six months later the vigilantes grabbed an ex-Sydney convict on suspicion of robbery. Trying him in their own kangaroo court, they found him guilty and promptly set about hanging him from a heavy wooden beam. Yelled Brannan, "Every lover of liberty and good order, lay hold of this rope!"

In 1856 James King, editor of the San Francisco *Bulletin,* exposed crooked politicians controlling the city's vice and crime. One enraged official, James P. Casey, shot and killed him. Friends rushed Casey off to jail to save him from being lynched. The vigilantes organized themselves into military companies and marched on the jail, where the sheriff quickly yielded up Casey and Charles Cora, a gambler also accused of murder. They were marched off and held overnight for a vigilante "trial."

Two hours after midnight, California's Governor Neely Johnson called personally at vigilante headquarters. Mob leaders told him that the vice ring controlled the city's courts, so that only they could be depended upon to punish murder. The governor shook their hands and said, "Go to it, then, but get through it as quickly as you can because there is terrible opposition and pressure." Several hours later, however, he returned with several officials, this time insisting that the prisoners must be turned over to the courts.

The vigilantes refused, tried the two men in a kangaroo court, and hanged them. Governor Johnson then declared the County of San Francisco to be in "a state of insurrection," and called upon all citizens to enlist in a militia under his friend General William Tecumseh Sherman to enforce martial law. But so popular was the support of the vigilantes that Johnson's order was ignored and Sherman resigned his command.

Vigilante extremism also flourished in frontier towns of the Middle and Far West. Rustlers and outlaws were hunted down by lynch mobs in the pay of the local power structure. Montana's notorious "Stranglers" hanged no less than sixty-three suspected cattle and horse rustlers, leaving them swinging from cottonwoods or cabin doors as warnings. "Not with the best judgment in all cases, however," admitted Theodore Roosevelt, who bought a ranch in the badlands before moving into the White House.

Marxist extremism made its first impact on Americans during the winter of 1851–52, when Horace Greeley serialized Karl Marx's book, *Revolution and Counter Revolution*, in the *Tribune*. Many German immigrants of that period were workers who believed in Marx's ideas. They were active in the labor move-ment of the 1850s, helping organize the National Typographic Union (1852), the United Hatters (1856), and the Iron Mould-ers' Union of North America (1859).

Marxist Socialists believed that just as a revolutionary bour-geoisie, or middle class, had overthrown feudalism by the indus-trial revolution, so the revolutionary proletariat, or working class, was destined to overthrow the bourgeoisie in turn by a Socialist revolution. A tiny band of extremists, they had few fol-lowers until later in the century.

The great acceleration of immigration during the 1840s pro-voked a strong resurgence of anti-alienism and anti-Catholicism. Small extremist groups like the Order of the Star-Spangled Ban-ner, the Order of United Americans, the American Protestant Society, and the American and Foreign Christian Union amal-gamated into a new secret society, the Native American Party. When asked about it, each member was sworn to reply, "I know nothing!" Horace Greeley derisively named them the Know-Nothings, and the name stuck. Few extremist movements in American history ever provoked more anarchy or wild disorder.

The first uproar came when President Franklin Pierce appointed Pennsylvania Attorney General James Campbell, a Catholic, as United States Postmaster General. The Know-Nothings held furious meetings to denounce the appointment for "putting all the secrets of American diplomacy in the Pope's hands."

They financed a renegade priest, Father Alessandro Gavazsi, on a lecture tour in 1853 to warn the country that "Satanical Jesuits . . . would ruin America if allowed." Every Catholic car-dinal, he charged, was really a spy and inquisitor for the Pope, sent to America "for the sole purpose of opposing, persecuting and fighting against the Protestant . . . community."

Riots that had to be broken up by troops firing their rifles broke out between Catholics and Know-Nothings.

The Know-Nothing movement agitated against Catholics in newspapers like Washington's *American Organ* and New York's *Herald,* and in street-corner speeches by demagogic preachers.

On May 7, 1854, J. S. Orr, who called himself "the Angel Gabriel," was rabble rousing on a Boston street corner when Irish American laborers from nearby rolling mills hurled missiles at him. They were driven off by goon squads of Know-Nothings, who then terrorized the neighborhood, smashing the windows of Catholic homes and the nearby church.

Three weeks later in New York a Know-Nothing street preacher inflamed a mob into marching on City Hall and assaulting anyone who "looked Irish." The next week, when another demagogue in Brooklyn attracted a street crowd of twenty thousand, the resulting riot between Catholics and Know-Nothings grew so fierce that police shots had no effect. The National Guard had to be called out to quell the disorder.

In that same long, hot summer of 1854, Know-Nothing mobs in Maine used battering rams to demolish the pews of a Catholic church, which they then burned. In St. Louis, Missouri, they started a whispering campaign to the effect that the Catholic college and St. Patrick's Church hid secret arsenals for arming the "papists." A mob wielding axes smashed fifty to sixty Irish American homes, seriously wounding many occupants.

"For forty-eight hours," reported the *St. Louis Evening News* on August 9, 1854, "the city has been the scene of one of the most appalling riots that has ever taken place in the country. Men have been butchered like cattle, property destroyed and anarchy reigns supreme. . . . The military and police have, thus far, been unable to check the onward march of lawlessness and crime. The scenes of last night were terrible, never, we hope, to be enacted again."

The Know-Nothings declared that German and Irish immigrants controlled city political machines and were stealing the elections.

The intolerance of the Know-Nothings succeeded in poisoning the minds of millions of Americans with anti-Catholic suspicion. Know-Nothing candidates won impressive strength at the polls, almost capturing New York, winning in Massachusetts, electing governors in nine states. In Congress, eight out of sixty-two senators and 104 out of 234 representatives were avowed Know-Nothings. Catholics and immigrants grew dismayed and frightened.

What had gone wrong in the promised land of religious liberty, of freedom, justice, and equality for all?

Anti-Catholic extremism flamed on all that year and the next. In Louisville, Kentucky, a Know-Nothing stronghold, Catholics were frightened away from the polls on election day, August 6, 1855, by knife-wielding mobs who attacked the Irish American quarter and burned down houses. In Ohio a Catholic church was blown up with gunpowder. In Maine a priest was tarred and feathered, then ridden out of town on a rail.

The Know-Nothings made a fatal blunder that summer at their national convention of the American Party. Southern extremists won control and passed pro-slavery resolutions, nominating ex-President Millard Fillmore, who had signed the Fugitive Slave Act, as their candidate for the White House.

A citizen of Springfield, Illinois, urged every abolitionist Know-Nothing to quit the American Party instantly.

"How can anyone who abhors the oppression of Negroes be in favor of degrading classes of white people?" wrote Abraham Lincoln in a letter on August 24, 1855. He added, "As a nation we began by declaring that 'all men are created equal.' We now practically read it, 'all men are created equal except Negroes.' When the Know-Nothings obtain control, it will read, 'All men are created equal except Negroes, foreigners and Catholics.'"

Abolitionists left the American Party in droves. The Know-Nothings frantically sought to replace their numbers by appealing to America's "mechanics" (factory workers) to join their fight against "cheap-working foreigners." But in the elections of 1856, they could poll only nine hundred thousand votes for Fillmore, who finished a poor third behind the Democratic winner, James Buchanan (1,927,000) and Republican John C. Fremont (1,391,000).

From then on Know-Nothing influence dwindled rapidly. Americans began dividing along regional, rather than religious, lines—North against South, free states versus slave states. In 1860, a dying force, the American Party merged with conservative Democrats and old-line Whigs into the Constitutional Union Party. It ran fourth in the four-way election contest that put Abraham Lincoln in the White House.

The most important extremists of the 1850s, of course, were those on the left and right of Lincoln's position on the slavery question. Slavery had its rabid defenders, like George Fitzhugh of Virginia who wrote in 1857, "The black slaves of the South are the happiest, and, in some sense, the freest people in the world." Fervently opposed to this view were the abolitionists whose Bible was Harriet Beecher Stowe's melodramatic but cataclysmic portrait of slavery, *Uncle Tom's Cabin.*

In abolitionist eyes, the only real extremists were the architects and supporters of a system that permitted white human beings to own and enslave black human beings.

Abolitionists who advocated an amicable solution to the problem, and Southern gradualists who were hopeful of compromise, were both crushed and obliterated between the slavery-haters who were convinced that only violence would free the slaves and slaveholders who were determined on revolt before emancipation.

American opinion rapidly polarized around both extremes.

9

Civil War Extremists, the K.K.K., and Indian-Killers

As a result of the uproar and controversy over *Uncle Tom's Cabin*, in 1853 the *New York Times* sent an unopinionated observer, Frederick Law Olmsted, subsequent designer of the city's Central Park, to travel through the South and send back purely factual reports of what he observed of the slave system.

In Virginia he attended a slave auction, watching a black woman put up for sale with an infant at her breast and two children at her side. "Well, gentlemen, here is a capital woman and her three children, all in good health—what do you say for them? Give me an offer. I put up the whole lot at $850 . . . A very extraordinary bargain, gentlemen. A fine, healthy baby. Hold it up. . . ." The next "lot" was a male slave who was ordered to strip behind a screen, whereupon a dozen buyers examined every part of him as they would a horse.

Olmsted's unemotional vignettes of what he saw in his Southern travels proved more shocking than Stowe's exaggerated fiction. The ranks of abolitionist extremists swelled.

At a huge Independence Day anti-slavery rally at Framingham, Massachusetts, in 1854, William Lloyd Garrison held aloft a copy of the Constitution and denounced it for failing to prohibit slavery. "The Constitution is a covenant with death and an agreement with Hell!" he shouted, setting fire to it.

The great crowd thundered its approval.

Northern and Southern extremists clashed bloodily in Kansas in a rehearsal of the civil war to come. Stephen A. Douglas's Kansas-Nebraska Act of 1854 brought on the fight by repealing the Missouri Compromise, which had guaranteed that this part of the Louisiana Territory would be forever free soil, and leaving it up to the settlers to decide for themselves.

Pro-slavery Missouri border gangs fought a guerrilla war with Northern free soil squatters for control of the territory. "Border ruffians" attacked the anti-slavery capital of Lawrence. Abolitionist John Brown countered with a savage raid on pro-slavery Pottawatomie, butchering five defenseless settlers.

The fever of extremism reached into the Senate. Following a defense of slavery by Senator Andrew P. Butler of South Carolina, an abolitionist, Charles Sumner of Massachusetts, rose to castigate Butler and charge, "The Nebraska Bill was in every respect a swindle . . . of the North by the South."

After adjournment for the day Sumner worked for awhile at his desk. Suddenly South Carolina Congressman Preston B. Brooks approached and said, "Mr. Sumner, you have libeled my state and slandered my relative, Senator Butler . . . and I feel it my duty to punish you for it!" Raising a heavy cane, he beat Sumner senseless in his seat. The South toasted Brooks as its hero of the hour. The North raged against Southern fanaticism.

No extremist was more fanatical than abolitionist John Brown, who turned up in Virginia with thirteen white and five black followers. He led them in a raid on the federal arsenal at Harper's Ferry to seize guns, arm Virginia's blacks, and lead a slave rebellion. The raiders killed the town's mayor and took leading citizens prisoner before they were overwhelmed by a Marine force led by Colonel Robert E. Lee.

Only Brown and four men were captured alive. Two of the dead were his own sons; Brown himself was wounded.

Abolitionists firmly championed Brown's view of himself as an avenging angel fighting in the service of the Lord. "I am only walking now as God foreordained I should walk," the old man with the flowing white beard said. "Let them hang me. I forgive them, and may God forgive them. For they know not what they do." But the South, and many Northern moderates as well, saw him as a revolutionist, a murderer, a bloody madman.

"A notorious Kansas horsethief," Stephen A. Douglas called him contemptuously, "a criminal who will rightly suffer on the gallows for his crimes." A Virginia legislator shouted, "The South must stand forth as one man and say to fanaticism in her own language—whenever you advance a hostile foot upon our soil, we will welcome you with bloody hands to hospitable graves!"

John Brown refused his counsel's urging that he plead insanity. A Virginia jury brought in a verdict of murder, criminal conspiracy, and treason. John Brown was sentenced to hang.

Mass meetings sprang up in churches and town halls all over the North. In one fiery speech Emerson dubbed Brown "the new saint . . . who will make the gallows glorious like the cross." Longfellow said, "They are leading John Brown to execution in Virginia. It will be . . . the date of a new Revolution—quite as much needed as the old one. This is sowing the wind to reap the whirlwind, *which will come soon!*" Greeley predicted, "I think the end of slavery in the Union is ten years nearer than it seemed a few weeks ago."

Abolitionist armies of up to sixteen thousand men were reported to be massing in cities all over the North, pledged to invade Virginia and rescue John Brown. Alarmed, Governor Henry Wise wired President Buchanan for help. Troops poured in to Charlestown to safeguard the execution on December 2, 1859.

From France, Victor Hugo observed, "The eyes of Europe are fixed on America. The hanging of John Brown will open a latent fissure that will finally split the Union asunder." It did.

Within eighteen months Northern troops were invading the South to the tune of *John Brown's Body*.

The Civil War reflected a collision of two extremist power structures that could no longer tolerate each other. There were moderates on both sides who deplored a war of Americans against Americans as the worst possible answer to the slavery problem. Even those staunchly committed to the Union cause acknowledged the savage war to be unbearable.

"Oh, my God it is horrible—horrible!" Greeley groaned in the spring of 1863. "How long must we go on killing each other?" On June 30, 1864, General Sherman wrote his brother grimly, "I begin to regard the death and mangling of a couple thousand men as a small affair, a kind of morning clash—and it may be well that we become so hardened."

In June 1863, following the bloody battle of Gettysburg, Northern revulsion set the stage for anti-war extremists. A giant peace rally was held at New York City's Cooper Union, with Mayor Fernando Wood as its chief speaker. There was indignation at a draft law that let rich men buy poor substitutes to serve for them. Irish American stevedores were furious because their strike for higher wages had been broken by freed slaves imported to New York.

The next month, anti-draft riots broke out in the city. For four days mobs raced through the streets smashing draft centers, lynching blacks, looting shops, overturning horsecars, wrecking saloons and burning the homes of the rich and the abolitionists. Several hundred people were killed and wounded before troops could restore order.

A different form of extremism characterized the power structure. Fortunes in war profits were made by Armour in meat packing, Weyerhauser in lumber, Huntington in railroads,

Remington in guns, Rockefeller in oil, Carnegie in iron and steel, Borden in milk, Marshall Field in merchandising. Many poor of North and South alike felt bitterly, not without reason, that the conflict was "a rich man's war and a poor man's fight."

Both sides of the Civil War were guilty of committing atrocities. When the Union began using black troops, the indignant Confederacy ordered that any white officer captured leading black troops must be executed. At the military prison at Andersonville, Georgia, over thirteen thousand out of fifty thousand Northern prisoners died, many of them victims of cruelty.

Equally extremist was Sherman's brutal march to the sea, cutting a sixty-mile swathe of destruction through Georgia that burned and demolished provisions, crops, cattle, cotton gins, bridges, and railroads, with looting attacks on homes that sent terrified Southerners fleeing into woods and swamps.

Few Presidents of American history were forced to endure more extremist vilification than Lincoln got from Northern dissidents. Called a drunkard, atheist, Socialist, bastard, part black and a baboon, he was compelled to deny before a Senate Committee that early military defeats in the war had been caused by a leakage of military secrets by his wife.

Harper's Weekly for September 1864, described him this way: "Filthy Story-Teller, Despot, Liar, Thief, Braggart, Buffoon, Usurper, Monster, Ignoramus Abe, Old Scoundrel, Perjurer, Robber, Swindler, Tyrant, Fiend, Butcher, Land-Pirate."

His Gettysburg Address, said the *Chicago Times,* was "an offensive exhibition of boorishness and vulgarity . . . a perversion of history." Lincoln sighed, "If to be head of Hell is as hard as what I have to undergo here, I could find it in my heart to pity Satan himself." But it was the South that produced the extremist to cut him down—John Wilkes Booth, the fanatical misfit actor who fancied himself in the melodramatic role of Brutus striking down a tyrannical Caesar.

Booth at first plotted with a group of Northern Copperheads—Southern sympathizers—to kidnap the President for the Confederacy. When this scheme fell through he decided on assassination. On the night of April 14, 1865, Lincoln sat with his wife and guests in a box at Ford's Theatre, Washington, watching a performance of *Our American Cousin*. Booth managed to enter the unguarded box and fire a single-shot Derringer at the back of the President's head. Crying, "Sic *semper tyrannis!*" (Ever thus to tyrants), he leaped down to the stage.

The jump broke his leg, but he managed to escape. Several days later he was cornered and shot. The Southern extremist press glorified Booth as a hero. "God almighty ordered this event," said the Dallas *Herald,* "or it could never have taken place." The Houston *Tri-Weekly Telegraph* said, "From now until God's judgment day, the minds of men will not cease to thrill at the killing of Abraham Lincoln."

Ironically, the anti-Lincoln extremists who hailed Booth's deed were applauding a turn of events that proved a postwar boomerang. Lincoln had intended to offer the South a magnanimous peace to bind up the country's wounds, declaring, "Government should not act for revenge." But his death left extremists of the Northern power structure free to indulge the popular clamor for revenge.

A glaring instance of Northern postwar extremism was the treatment of Jefferson Davis, President of the Confederacy. Unjustly blamed for plotting Lincoln's assassination, he was the target of President Andrew Johnson's angry offer of a hundred thousand dollars for his capture. News of Booth's deed reached Davis as he was fleeing south with his cabinet from Richmond.

"If it is true," he told his colleagues, "then we have lost our only refuge. Mr. Lincoln would have been much more useful to the South than Andrew Johnson is likely to be."

He was captured by Union soldiers at Irwinville, Georgia, on May 10, 1865, and taken to Fort Monroe. Losing his temper when served miserable rations, he flung them at the corporal who brought them. Major General Nelson A. Miles ordered him put in leg-irons. It took four soldiers to shackle the outraged Confederate President. Five days later Secretary of War Edwin M. Stanton ordered the leg-irons removed.

But Davis was kept locked in a fort cell, guarded day and night, for five months. General Miles proudly exhibited him to visitors as though he were a rare captive tiger.

For two years Davis was kept imprisoned, awaiting a trial that never came because President Johnson knew that there was no evidence linking him to Lincoln's assassination. It was Horace Greeley, sickened by these "harsh and needless indignities," who finally led a group of twenty prominent Americans, including abolitionist Gerrit Smith, to demand that the Government free Davis on bail they had raised. Two years later an embarrassed government dropped all charges against him.

Northern extremism also made itself felt during the Reconstruction Period, although Southern firebrands often exaggerated the extent to which unscrupulous Northern carpetbaggers used ignorant freed slaves to clamp a rule of humiliation and tyranny on defeated Southern whites.

There were, indeed, many instances of injustice in the military and political control that the Radical Republicans imposed upon the South. Often corrupt state governments were kept in power only by federal bayonets. But many of the South's shattered schools, hospitals, and other institutions were rebuilt through private Northern philanthropy.

Extremists in the Southern power structure played into the hands of the Radical Republicans by refusing to recognize that the war had settled the slavery question. Instead they passed "black codes" to "keep the black in his place."

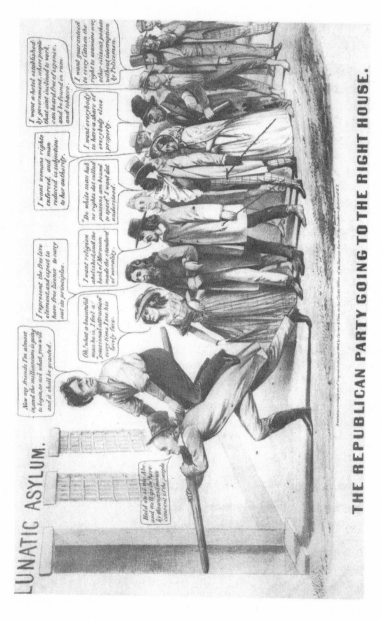

As this Currier and Ives cartoon shows, Abraham Lincoln was the target of a multitude of extremist groups.

A Canadian journalist, John Richard Bennett, described in *The Nation* an 1865 visit to the Virginia Bureau of Freedmen when two Mississippi planters called to hire a hundred black cotton hands. They were shocked at being told that the Bureau had no power to order them to go unless they wanted to, and that they could not be compelled to work once they got there.

"But I *know* the black," protested one planter. "The employer must have some sort of punishment. I don't care what it is. If you'll let me tie him up by the thumbs, or keep him on bread and water, that will do. Over here in Rockbridge County, I saw a black tied up by the wrists. His hands were way up above his head. I went along to him, and says I, 'Boy, which would you like best now, to stay there where you are, or to have me take you down, give you forty good cuts, and let you go?' 'Rather have the forty lash,' says he. So he would, too. You folks used to make a good deal of talk because we gave our blacks a flogging when they deserved it!"

Embittered Confederate soldiers returned home to find themselves confronted by a situation that seemed to them intolerable. The slaves, whom they had looked down upon as inferior beasts of burden, were now a legally free majority in some states, entitled to vote on equal terms with the white men who had only recently owned them. Many whites dreaded that the blacks would use their new rights vengefully.

Before the war many whites had belonged to secret terror societies like Knights of the Golden Circle, Knights of the Columbian Order, and The Minutemen, lynching or flogging Southern whites suspected of opposing slavery or secession. In 1866 a group of young Confederate veterans of Pulaski, Tennessee, formed a new order of fanatical racists called the Ku Klux Klan (KKK), after the Greek word *kuklos* (band or circle).

Similar Klans quickly sprang up all over the South. Klansmen spread terror among former slaves to keep them from claiming their new rights. Wearing long white robes, masks, and pointed hoods, they flogged, beat, and murdered blacks, and also threatened white Reconstruction officials. Depicting themselves as gallant "knights" defending the purity of white womanhood, they sought to reestablish white supremacy.

At Nashville in 1867 the various state Klans met in a secret convention and amalgamated as the Invisible Empire of the South. Officials were exalted by bizarre nomenclature. The Grand Wizard of the Empire had ten Genii as assistants; Grand Dragons of the Realm had their Hydras; Grand Titans of the Dominions had Furies for aides; and Grand Giants of the Province were assisted by their Goblins.

Riding at night with whips, pistol, and rope, Klansmen forced blacks to withdraw from the political life of the South. Flaming crosses, Klan symbols, were planted in the front yards of those they wished to frighten. Anyone interfering with, or exposing, their crimes was murdered. Homes of anti-Klan Southerners were burned down. In Mississippi, schools for blacks were destroyed and their teachers driven off. Night rallies of the hooded mobs, visible on hills in the light of huge burning crosses, intensified the climate of terror.

Brawley Gilmore, an illiterate Union, South Carolina, black man, recalled years later, "When I was a boy on the Gilmore place, the Ku Klux would come along at night a-riding the colored folks like they was goats. Yes, sir, they had em down on all fours acrawling, and they would be on their backs. They would carry them to Turk Creek bridge and make them set up on the bannisters, then they would shoot 'em offen the bannisters into the water. I 'clare them was the awfulest days I ever is seed."

The Klan often left victims hanging from trees for four or five days to frighten others, and shot anyone who dared take them down. Forbidden Christian burial in graveyards, victims were often simply dumped into pits and covered over.

In 1868 a Congressional investigation found that in just three weeks prior to election day, two thousand people had been murdered, wounded, or flogged in Louisiana. In twenty-nine counties of Georgia that year there had been seventy-two racial murders and 126 floggings; in fourteen counties of North Carolina, eighteen murders and 315 floggings. Congress branded the Klan "a fearful conspiracy" that had "demoralized society, and held men silent by the terror of its acts and by its powers for evil."

Among the extremists denounced were important figures of the Southern power structure—Grand Wizard, General Nathaniel B. Forrest; Georgia Grand Dragon, General John B. Gordon; North Carolina Grand Dragon, ex-governor Zebulon B. Vance.

In 1871 President Ulysses S. Grant ordered the Ku Klux Klan disbanded. Hundreds of Klansmen were arrested under an act of Congress (later declared unconstitutional) that permitted the President to declare martial law and jail citizens of organizations he considered to be in rebellion against the government. But the Southern power structure continued to intimidate blacks by passing "Jim Crow" state laws that prevented them from exercising their civil rights.

As American expansion pushed westward after the Civil War, a new form of extremism materialized known as "civilizing the West." Behind this euphemism lay the goal of confiscating Indian lands for pioneer settlement. Many pioneers were racist Southerners who refused to remain in an emancipated South, and took their prejudices against non-white races west with them.

Scorned as "colored barbarians," the Indians were also swept aside by Northern troops reflecting the Establishment's determination that all land between the Mississippi and the West Coast must come under white settlement and control. The Indians fought back desperately. Their ferocity in battle was matched by the atrocities often committed by white invaders against Indian men, women, and children.

The Indians had already been swept forcibly out of their Eastern lands. In 1828 President Andrew Jackson, an old Indian fighter, put the Indian Removal Act through Congress forcing all tribes to migrate west of the Mississippi. Even before this, when gold had been found in the Cherokee country of Georgia, the state Legislature had passed a law confiscating all Cherokee lands within the state, nullifying all laws of the Cherokee Nation, and forbidding Indians to testify in court against white men. The Supreme Court turned a deaf ear to Cherokee appeals.

Three indignant white missionaries living in the Cherokee Nation refused to swear oaths of allegiance to Georgia. Arrested, they were chained together for a twenty-one-mile march, then sentenced to four years at hard labor. Two Methodist preachers who protested were similarly persecuted.

General Winfield Scott, future hero of the Mexican War, invaded the Cherokee Nation with seven thousand troops. Seizing Indian men, women, and children, he marched them off to Arkansas concentration camps in midwinter. Their lands and possessions were divided among whites by lottery. Of fourteen thousand Cherokees herded onto a "trail of tears" reminiscent of the Bataan death march over a century later, four thousand died on the way.

Horace Greeley bitterly labeled the United States Indian Bureau as "murderers." But in 1871 General Francis C. Walker, then Commissioner of Indian Affairs, declared, "When dealing with savage men, as with savage beasts, no question of national honor can arise. Whether to fight, to run away, or to employ a ruse, is solely a question of expediency." John Collier, a later Commissioner (1933–1945), summed up the extremist policies of his predecessors bluntly and tersely: "The white conqueror . . . pronounced sentence of death on the Indian societies."

Power structure propaganda persuaded white American Western "fans," and children playing cowboys and Indians, that cowboys were always the "good guys," Indians, the "bad guys." Every child learned that Indians scalped their victims; but few were informed about Indian families slaughtered in their tents by United States cavalry raids. Custer's defeat in the Battle of Little Big Horn of 1876 was pictured to Americans as the massacre of a hero and his men, but a real massacre of Indians in 1890 was designated the Battle of Wounded Knee.

The original Americans were driven out of their lands, rounded up in open-air concentration camps, killed by troops when they strayed off these reservations, cheated by traders, often shot on sight by pioneers. Their food was stolen by the commercial buffalo-hunters, their plains, confiscated and fenced in by the cattle ranchers.

On February 4, 1874, General Sherman and three other generals, designated by Congress as a commission to investigate the cause of the Indian wars, testified before the House Committee on Indian Affairs. They reported their finding that nine out of ten Indian outbreaks had been provoked by the outrages of white extremists or Washington's broken promises.

"The Indians are robbed constantly," General William S. Harney, a veteran Indian fighter, testified. "I know it of my own knowledge. That is the principal cause of Indian difficulties. In fact, if we would keep our treaty stipulations with the Indians we would have no trouble with them. The Indians do not violate their treaty stipulations, except when they are driven to it by the whites."

And so "civilization" was brought to the West.

10

Monopolists, Bomb-Throwers, and Saloon-Wreckers

Following the Civil War, industrialists who had prospered by it sought to build trade empires. Using extremist methods, they formed trusts to eliminate competition and charge any prices they liked. One combine known as the Big Six controlled street railways in over a hundred Eastern cities, and also held a gas and electric light monopoly in eighty of them. In New York City the infamous Tweed Ring plundered 100 million dollars in less than three years by a combine of crooked officials and businessmen.

The shrewdest monopolist of all was John D. Rockefeller, of whom satirist "Mr. Dooley" (Peter Dunne) said: "He's a kind iv a society fr th' previntion iv cruelty to money. If he finds a man misusin' his money, he takes it way fr'm him an' adopts it." In the late 1870s Rockefeller secretly negotiated midnight contracts to form a trust with his Standard Oil Company and the nation's fifteen biggest oil refiners. "We mean to secure the entire refining business of the world," he told them, and warned them to conceal trust profits.

The public grew indignant as it became aware of the unscrupulous methods Rockefeller used to force any company refusing to buy from Standard Oil out of business. In 1879 he and the other big business extremists were indicted for criminal conspiracy "to secure a monopoly of the oil industry, to oppress other refiners . . . to fraudulently control prices."

When the Ohio courts ordered his trust dissolved, Rockefeller simply reincorporated it as a holding company under the more generous laws of New Jersey. By 1900 he had eliminated all major competitors and amassed a tremendous fortune.

In 1905 he was a prime target for the "muckrakers"—crusading magazine reporters out to expose extremism in the power structure. In *McClure's Magazine,* Ida M. Tarbell wrote, "He is a victim of perhaps the ugliest . . . of all passions, that for money. . . . This money-maniac secretly, patiently, eternally plotting how he may add to his wealth . . . points to his church-going and his charities as proof of his righteousness. . . . There is but one name for it—hypocrisy."

In 1914, the Rockefeller family, concerned about such indictments, hired a public relations expert, Ivy Lee, to erase the stigma attached to the Rockefeller reputation. Lee advised establishing the now-famous Rockefeller Foundation, and worked to change Rockefeller's public image to that of a kindly, thrifty, rather humorous old rich man who patted little boys on the head, gave them dime tips, and used his great wealth for philanthropy.

Other monopolists included Armour and Swift who, with two other packers, formed a beef trust; Guggenheim, who forged a copper monopoly; and Duke, who set up a tobacco trust. A survey in 1904 showed that 319 trusts had swallowed up 5,300 businesses, and 127 utilities had wiped out the competition of 2,400 companies. The average man found himself gouged by higher prices for food, clothes, homes, furnishings, transportation, light, fuel, matches, whiskey and badly-needed loans.

In 1884 growing public anger produced a National Anti-Monopoly Party, but the Democratic nominee for President, Grover Cleveland, quickly stole their thunder by denouncing the big corporations as "the people's masters." In 1890 a

"Father, dear Father, come home!"

This cartoon ridicules the American government's toleration of the detested monopolies.

reluctant Congress passed the Sherman Anti-Trust Act outlawing monopolies. But corrupt or prejudiced judges kept the law from being enforced against the big corporations. Instead, they used it against labor unions, which were indicted as "conspiracies in restraint of trade."

Among the earliest labor extremists were the Molly Maguires, a secret terrorist association of Irish American miners in Pennsylvania, named after an Irish society that assaulted agents of their hated absentee landlords. The American Mollies attacked mine superintendents, bosses, and company police; they also blew up collieries. During the Civil War over fifty violent murders by the Mollies went unpunished because no one on the coalfields dared testify against them.

In 1873 James McParlan joined the Mollies, and in two years became popular enough to be made a lodge officer. Then the Mollies were stunned when scores of them were suddenly arrested for murder on the testimony of McParlan, who proved to be a Pinkerton spy hired by the Philadelphia and Reading Coal and Iron Company. Ten Mollies were executed; fourteen more went to prison. The organization fell apart.

There were thirty-seven thousand strikes between 1881 and 1905, a period of great labor unrest. Many were violent, caused by extremism on both sides. Workers sometimes pressed their demands with fists, clubs, stones, weapons, and torches. Anger at the company and a hungry family at home often created a mood of desperation, as did the conviction that the whole power structure was united in a conspiracy against them.

Extremist industrialists were also responsible for labor violence. Some hired thugs to break up a union's picket line, meetings, or demonstrations. Others sought to break strikes by importing scab labor. Still others used *agents provocateurs* to sabotage company property in order to discredit strikers, as during the railroad strikes of 1867. Carroll D. Wright, US Commissioner of Labor, testified that agents for the Vanderbilt-owned Pennsylvania Railroad had set fire to worthless freight cars in Pittsburgh to blame the union and give the company a pretext for calling out troops to crush the strike.

The two largest national labor unions of the 1880s—Knights of Labor and the American Federation of Labor (AFL)—were anything but extremist. The Knights preferred the boycott to the strike; the AFL's Samuel Gompers concentrated on monopolizing the supply of skilled craftsmen with the power to tie up a company's production if forced to strike.

The real extremists in labor's ranks were radicals who were few in number but influential, like a German anarchist, Johann Most, a veteran of prisons in Berlin, Vienna, and London. In addition to editing the German-language paper, *Freiheit,* in New York City, he published a handbook, *The Science of Revolutionary Warfare,* teaching how to make dynamite bombs.

"Dynamite!" wrote Most enthusiastically. "Of all the good stuff, that is the stuff! Stuff several pounds . . . in the vicinity of a lot of rich loafers who live by the sweat of other people's brows, and light the fuse. A most cheerful and gratifying result will follow." Most's ideas strongly influenced a tiny radical group in Chicago called the International Working People's Party, through a paper called *The Alarm* edited by Albert Parsons, who had previously run for mayor on the Socialist Labor ticket.

Chicago workers of the McCormick Reaper Works went out on strike in 1886. When the company locked them out on May 3 and brought in scab labor to replace them, a riot ensued. Six strikers were killed in a shooting fray with police. Hours later leaflets flooded the streets saying: "REVENGE! WORKING-MEN TO ARMS!" The next day a mass protest meeting gathered in Haymarket Square, where over three thousand strikers, Socialists, trade unionists, and anarchists heard a speaker urge them to violence.

When police tried to break them up, someone suddenly threw a dynamite bomb. After a blinding flash, sixty police lay injured and another seven were dead. Other police opened fire on the crowd, wounding many of the demonstrators.

An extremist response by the power structure was swift. Meeting secretly, three hundred industrial leaders organized a Citizens' Association with a hundred thousand dollar fund to "suppress anarchy." A press campaign inflamed public hysteria over bomb-throwing anarchists. Police staged raids on union headquarters, arresting hundreds of workers on suspicion. When seven were arraigned as anarchists, Albert Parsons emerged voluntarily from hiding to stand trial with them. None was proved guilty of having either made or hurled the Haymarket bomb.

Nevertheless Parsons and three workers were hanged; a fourth committed suicide in his cell; three others were given life sentences. In 1893 Illinois Governor John P. Altgeld pardoned them for having been illegally sentenced by a prejudiced judge and jury in an unfair trial ruled by mob hysteria.

"This lying, hypocritical, demagogical, sniveling Governor of Illinois does not want the laws enforced," raged the *Chicago Tribune.* "He is a sympathizer with riot, with violence, with lawlessness and with anarchy. He should be impeached. . . . He has put Illinois to shame." Such demagogic attacks ended Altgeld's political career.

The power structure used the Haymarket affair first to inflame public fear of anarchists, then to equate lawlessness with strikes. Labor itself split bitterly between extremists advocating militancy, and conservatives and moderates who urged peaceful education of the public to workers' rights.

The idealistic Knights of Labor perished in the turmoil. Sam Gompers strengthened the AFL by tightening his monopoly on skilled labor to meet the monopoly of big capital. Labor radicals gained influence in many of the strikes sweeping across the country, especially as the power structure turned increasingly to extremist measures to break strikes.

The first great labor battle of the era took place at Homestead, Pennsylvania, in July 1892. The Iron & Steel Workers Union called a strike when Henry Clay Frick, President of the Carnegie Steel Company, slashed wages despite company profits of four million dollars a year. Frick shut the plant down, locked out its 3,800 workers, and surrounded the works with a high fence that had firing holes for armed guards posted behind it.

He was determined to destroy the union at all plants of the monopolistic Carnegie empire. When he was ready to reopen the Homestead works with scab labor, two tugs came down river bringing three hundred armed Pinkerton men in blue uniforms to guard them and the plant. Strikers raced to the riverfront with their own weapons. Open warfare broke out, involving the use of cannon and dynamite. Several barges were set on fire.

The strikers won, but not until 163 men had been seriously wounded and fourteen killed. For five days they commanded the town and the steel works. Then state troops moved in, recaptured the plant, and restored order. This time a shocked public turned its anger primarily against extremist Henry Clay Frick and the Carnegie Steel Company.

Illinois Senator John McCauley Palmer attacked Frick for hiring "private mercenary armies" against workers who had every right to resist "in defense of their jobs and homes." Palmer sent shudders through the power structure by insisting that workers had just as much of a property right in their jobs as corporations had in their plants.

But public sympathy was alienated sixty-seven days after the Homestead war when anarchist Alexander Berkman, a Polish-Russian immigrant, suddenly burst into Frick's office and tried to assassinate him with a combination of gun, knife, and fulminate of mercury explosive. An incredible bungler, he only wounded Frick, who displayed cool nerves and courage as he grappled with and captured his assailant. Police found Berkman to be a fanatic from New York with no ties whatever to the union.

But that night Frick quickly told reporters that even if "they" killed him, he intended to operate all Carnegie plants with non-union crews. The press applauded his personal courage, and treated Berkman's crackpot act as a union plot. On November 21, Frick jubilantly cabled Andrew Carnegie, who had prudently stayed abroad all through the trouble: "STRIKE OFFICIALLY DECLARED OFF YESTERDAY. OUR VICTORY IS NOW COMPLETE AND MOST GRATIFYING. DO NOT THINK WE WILL EVER HAVE ANY SERIOUS LABOR TROUBLE AGAIN, . . . WE HAVE TAUGHT OUR EMPLOYEES A LESSON THAT THEY WILL NEVER FORGET."

Carnegie cabled back: "CONGRATULATIONS ALL AROUND. LIFE WORTH LIVING AGAIN. HOW PRETTY ITALIA."

Extremism in late nineteenth century economic conflicts was mirrored by extremism in the era's moral conflicts as well. Many women reformers involved in the struggle for equal rights and the vote were also crusaders in the campaign against "the demon rum." Drinking had always been a problem in America, but following the Civil War saloons increased at such a rapid rate that by 1900 most big cities had a saloon—"the poor man's club"— for every two hundred inhabitants.

A Prohibition Party was organized in 1869 to try to outlaw the sale of intoxicating beverages, but made little headway against the political influence of powerful brewers. So Frances Willard, President of the National Women's Christian Temperance Union (WCTU), decided to take extremist action to put the saloons out of business.

She began leading her followers into crowded saloons, where they knelt on the sawdust floors and sang hymns, praying for the deliverance of the American family from alcohol. Thousands of abashed barflies were awed into signing a pledge of abstinence and leaving with the women for church.

In 1874, Miss Willard's crusaders drove saloons out of business in 250 towns and villages of Ohio and neighboring states. When Cincinnati brewers drenched them with a fire hose and had them arrested, they marched to jail singing hymns. The WCTU's campaign won them new branches all over the nation. By 1895 an even more militant prohibitionist group was leading the battle—the Anti-Saloon League of America.

The brewers were hit in 1900 by a one-woman cyclone named Carrie Nation. A prohibitionist driven by the apostolic zeal of a Nat Turner or John Brown, she heard a heavenly voice direct her, "Go to Kiowa! Take something in your hands and throw it at those places and smash them!" Kiowa, twenty miles from her abode in Medicine Lodge, Kansas, was considered the "wettest" town in the county. So Carrie filled her buggy with stones and bricks and kept her rendezvous with destiny.

Carrying an armful of missiles, she entered a saloon and told astonished imbibers at the bar, "Men, I have come to save you from a drunkard's fate!" *Wham! Crash!* The bar mirror shattered, and every glass on the back bar went next. Then well-aimed pitches took care of every bottle in view.

"Now, Mr. Dobson," she told the thunderstruck saloon-owner, "I have finished. God be with you." As an afterthought, when she drove off she tossed two bricks through his plate glass windows. Then she demolished two more saloons before the horrified mayor of Kiowa raced up to stop her. When he refused her request to be jailed, she drove off calmly.

Now she decided to dry up the whole state of Kansas.

Entering Wichita's elegant Hotel Carey, she approached its long, curved bar carrying a heavy iron rod and a supply of stones wrapped in newspaper. The bartender frowned.

"Sorry, madam, but we do not serve ladies."

"Serve *me*!" she screeched. "Do you think I'd drink your hellish poison?" She began smashing bottles. "Glory to God! Peace on earth, good will to men!" She had just cracked the $1,500 bar mirror when a detective rushed in.

"You're under arrest for defacing property."

"Defacing nothing!" she shouted. "I am *destroying!*"

She was released on bail, and then charges were dropped because the prosecutor expressed doubts about her sanity. But requests from all over the country urged Carrie to carry on.

Her next target was Topeka. Armed with newly-purchased hatchets, she and two female followers entered the city's Senate Bar and set to work chopping up the costly bar. Outraged, bartender Benner Tucker leveled a revolver and ordered them out. Carrie Nation lunged at him, swinging her hatchet.

With a howl of fright he fired two shots into the ceiling to bring police, then fled. Carrie swept every bottle and glass off the bar and back bar with her hatchet, cut the rubber tubing of the beer barrels and hosed the walls and ceiling with beer. The arrest of the three intemperate temperance crusaders made front pages all over the nation.

Carrie's notoriety inspired dozens of other hatchet-wielding extremists to smash up saloons in other states. She led another score of hatchet raids herself, but the public began to grow bored with her fanaticism. When she attacked a saloon in Montana, the owner proved to be a young and muscular lady who flattened Carrie with a few punches.

The WCTU ignored her as an embarrassment, and she began to be laughed at as an eccentric. Her lectures against saloons drew increasingly dwindling audiences. When she spoke in England, she was showered with eggs and vegetables.

But when she died, discredited, in 1911, prohibition was only seven years away, not only because of the respectable crusading of the WCTU and Anti-Saloon League, but perhaps even more because of the publicity won by the extremist Carrie Nation.

11

"By George and By Jingo!"

Enthusiastic Californians anticipated a great boom in population and prosperity to follow the link-up of the Union Pacific and Central Pacific. But many were startled and upset by an article called "What the Railroad Will Bring Us" in the *Overland Monthly*. The railroad, wrote journalist Henry George, would bring "wealth for the few and great poverty for the many."

As a region grew populous, he explained, land steadily increased in value. Soaring rents enriched a few landlords but impoverished all their tenants. George demanded a tax based on the increase of land value since purchase, because landlords had done nothing to earn or deserve this gain, which resulted from the decision of people to populate an area.

He called it the Single Tax, insisting that if it were passed, no other taxes would be necessary. Owners of real estate and property reacted with understandable horror. Such a tax would in most cases amount to more than the rent received. The net effect would be to make all land communal property. The outraged power structure in California quickly induced the creditors of a newspaper George edited to foreclose it.

Seeking to develop his Single Tax policy into the basis for a new labor party, he wrote a book called *Progress and Poverty*. When it appeared in 1880, it was largely ignored. Moving to New York, he found great agitation among the city's Irish Americans over the landlord problem in Ireland. He wrote a pamphlet called *The Irish Land Question,* offering his Single Tax idea as the solution. Overnight he found himself a hero of the landlord-hating Irish Americans. Soon his book, too, began to be read widely and to make converts.

New York's labor unions, disgusted with the city's corrupt Democratic administration, united behind Henry George in 1886 as their reform candidate for mayor. He was given a good chance of winning until the Haymarket explosion soured public feeling toward labor. He was defeated, but beat the Republican candidate, twenty-eight-year-old Theodore Roosevelt.

When he died in 1897, his body lay in state at Grand Central Palace in New York City, and over a hundred thousand mourners filed by the coffin. Many wept for the radical who had insisted that the power structure had no right to permit poverty for the workers while the idle rich grew richer simply by owning land.

Far more extremist about the land than the Single Taxers were those who actually worked it—the farmers of the South, the West, and principally the Midwest. They grew increasingly alienated from the power structure as they failed to share in the economic boom of the last half of the nineteenth century.

"The fruits of the toil of millions are boldly stolen to build up colossal fortunes for a few," charged Minnesota farm politician Ignatius Donnelly. "From the same prolific womb of governmental injustice we breed the two great classes—tramps and millionaires." He warned, "The railroad corporations will either own the people or the people must own the railroads."

The farmers organized first into the Greenback Party, demanding cheap money with which to pay off their mortgages and debts. Failing at the polls, they formed the Farmers' Alliance to pressure Congress for farm support laws. Between 1890 and 1892 the alliance grew into the Populist Party, allying farmers with Knights of Labor, suffragettes, Socialists, Single Taxers and other discontented minorities.

Populist Mary Ellen Lease, known as "the Kansas Pythoness," traveled around the plains urging farmers to "raise less corn and more hell." She told them, "Wall Street owns the country. It is no longer a government of the people, by the people, for the people, but a government of Wall Street, by Wall Street, and for Wall Street. Our laws are the output of a system that clothes rascals in robes and honesty in rags!"

Her fiery speeches helped elect Senator William Peffer, a long-bearded Kansan denounced by Theodore Roosevelt as "a well-meaning, pinheaded, anarchistic crank."

Openly and belligerently extremist, the Populists demanded a new Declaration of Independence. "The history of the United States for the past twenty-eight years," they declared, "is a history of repeated injuries, tyranny, and usurpation, unparalleled in the history of the world, and all laws enacted . . . establish a money aristocracy on the ruins of a once free America."

They agitated for government ownership of railroads, telegraph, and telephone lines; cheap money through free coinage of silver on an equal par with gold; a ban on absentee ownership; a graduated income tax to make the rich pay more; restriction of immigration to stop the supply of cheap scab labor for big business; an eight-hour day for wage-earners; postal savings banks; the secret Australian ballot to end vote frauds; government warehouses where farmers could sell crops in exchange for 80 percent of their value in treasury notes.

"Socialism!" roared the Eastern press. But within the next generation, as Populists proved the popularity of their demands at the polls, both major parties quickly adopted many of these planks for their own campaigns.

The elections of 1890 swept Populists into power in a dozen Southern and Western states, sending many to Congress as well.

In 1892 their Presidential candidate, James B. Weaver, polled over a million votes against a combined eleven million votes for the two major parties. In 1896 the alarmed Democrats eliminated the Populist Party threat by absorbing it.

Their candidate, William Jennings Bryan, ran on the Populist platform of free silver—"You shall not press down upon the brow of labor the crown of thorns, you shall not crucify mankind upon a cross of gold." When he was defeated, he took the Populist cause down with him.

Anti-Catholic prejudice, latent since the demise of the Know-Nothings, flared up again in the late 1880s with the growing prestige, prosperity, and influence of American Catholics in the big cities. Small-town Protestants were also angered by scandals involving Irish American political bosses.

On March 13, 1887, seven men led by Henry F. Bowers organized the American Protective Association (APA) in Clinton, Iowa. In seven years they had seventy thousand members and seventy weeklies flooding the nation with anti-Catholic propaganda. They forged documents and fabricated wild stories like the one blaming Lincoln's assassination on a "Jesuit plot by Rome." Catholics were alleged to be drilling secretly at night in churches to take over America in a war against Protestants.

The APA demanded that Catholics be forbidden to vote, teach in public schools, recruit nuns for "a lecherous priesthood," or join the United States Army or Navy which, they charged, was already "Romanized." Anti-Catholic riots were touched off by the inflammatory speeches of APA street corner demagogues. Small-town vigilantes armed with Winchesters were stirred into invading Catholic churches to search for hidden arms.

The Reverend Washington Gladden, a leading Protestant minister who investigated APA charges and found them wholly spurious, urged fellow clergy, "For the honor of Protestantism, is it not high time to separate ourselves from this class of 'patriots'? In any large town, if the leading Protestant clergymen will speak out clearly, the plague will be stayed."

In 1896 the APA was still powerful enough to have a million members, overturning political regimes in eleven states and electing twenty representatives to Congress. It finally split itself apart, however, in a fight over whether to support Republican presidential nominee William McKinley, whose close friends and backers were Catholic.

The APA furor dwindled away into insignificance with the excitement that accompanied the Spanish-American War.

The extremist who first had the idea of marching on Washington in a protest demonstration was Jacob S. Coxey of Massillon, Ohio, a Greenbacker and Populist who owned a stone quarry. The year 1894 opened with the nation in the grip of a dismal depression. Factories were closed, three million were jobless, there were breadlines in the cities, homes were foreclosed, and farmers had to burn unsold corn for fuel.

Coxey had a plan for giving men jobs and putting the country back on its feet. He wanted the United States Treasury to issue 500 million dollars to finance good roads throughout the country, employing all idle men at $1.50 an hour for an eight-hour day. This high wage scale would compel private industry to match it. Result: full employment, a general eight-hour day, excellent transportation, new purchasing power, and a return of prosperity.

Coxey's idea was to find a responsive echo forty years later in the Works Project Administration (WPA) set up under the New Deal program of President Franklin D. Roosevelt.

To pressure the Congress of 1894 to act on his plan to aid the jobless, Coxey decided to lead a march on the national capital. Unemployed marchers were to come from all over the country, joining him for a monster demonstration in front of the Capitol at noon on May 1. Commissioning himself "General" Coxey, he announced that when his "Army of the Commonwealth of Christ" converged on Washington, it would number over a hundred thousand. News media gave the story front-page headlines.

On March 25, riding in a carriage, he led a small column of ragged men on foot out of Massillon. They picked up recruits daily as they wound toward their target. In California a contingent of a thousand hopped eastbound Union Pacific freight trains. Other "divisions" set out from big cities of the West and Midwest. Some stole trains at gunpoint, terrorizing small towns en route with gunplay. Hundreds were jailed; thousands never reached the East Coast.

Coxey's timing proved bad. He reached Washington on April 30; his only forces, the five hundred men behind him. He tried to speak from the Capitol steps but was charged by Washington police. When he and his aides were knocked over into the shrubbery, the crowd booed and yelled threats. The police swung clubs, trampling down and beating fifty marchers.

Coxey, treated as a crackpot, was arrested for "walking on the grass" in the Capitol grounds. He was fined five dollars and sentenced to twenty days in jail. His request for a hearing before a Congressional committee was denied. The press lost interest and Coxey's moment in the limelight faded, his protest movement reduced to a footnote in history.

Public attention switched to a new development in the headlines—the Chicago strike of Pullman workers that threatened to tie up all train travel. During the depression of 1893 George Pullman, president of the company, had slashed his workers' wages by as much as 40 percent, while voting stockholders, including Vanderbilt and Marshall Field, an 8 percent dividend. Pullman workers were already embittered by being compelled to live in the company's "model village," a company town where they had to buy in company stores.

Over 4,500 workers, earning an average $613 a year, were overcharged for rent, gas, and water. They were indebted to the company for over $70,000. Prices charged them stayed up when the wages paid them went down. Many testified later before a special commission, appointed by President Grover Cleveland, that when deductions had been made from their paychecks, many received a balance of under fifty cents a week.

"We were born," one worker said bitterly, "in a Pullman house, fed from the Pullman shop, taught in the Pullman school, catechized in the Pullman church, and when we die we shall be buried in the Pullman cemetery and go to the Pullman hell!"

The workers chose a grievance committee to appeal to Pullman to rescind the wage cuts. He fired the committee. On May 11, 1894, three thousand desperate Pullman employees went out on strike, appealing to Eugene Debs, the president of the new American Railway Union (ARU) to help them. Debs asked for arbitration.

"There is nothing to arbitrate," Pullman replied coldly. He explained why later to the President's commission: "Because it would violate . . . the principle that a man should have the right to manage his own property." Debs accused him of counting on "a little starvation" to bring his workers to their knees. On June 26, Debs ordered the ARU not to handle any trains carrying Pullman sleeping cars.

The boycott crippled major railroad operations in twenty-seven states, virtually paralyzing lines in the Middle and Far West. Angered railroad tycoons rallied to Pullman's side through a General Managers Association representing twenty-four lines. To crush Debs, the ARU, and the Pullman strikers, they used every resource available to the power structure—press, police, courts, and federal troops. The label of extremist was pinned not on Pullman for keeping his workers in peonage, but on Eugene Debs for coming to their defense. Newspapers controlled by the General Managers Association began mobilizing public opinion against Debs for mounting a "conspiracy" against the United States.

"War of the bloodiest kind in Chicago is imminent," said the *Washington Post* on July 7, "and before tomorrow goes by the railroad lines and yards may be turned into battlefields strewn with hundreds of dead and wounded." Another paper denounced Debs for leading "a war against the government and against society." When the General Managers Association hired strikebreakers to provoke fights, and *agents provocateurs* to set fire to ancient freight cars in the Chicago yards, the press obligingly reported that "insurrection and mob rule by strikers" had created a reign of terror in the city.

The power structure then signaled United States Attorney General Richard Olney, a former railroad counsel, to get a court injunction against the strike for "obstructing the railroads and holding up the mails." Olney talked President Cleveland into sending federal troops into Chicago to "restore order."

In the clashes that followed, twenty strikers were killed. On July 10, Debs and other union leaders were indicted for "conspiracy to obstruct the mails" and refusal to obey the court injunction. Despite Governor John B. Altgeld's appalled protest, Debs went to jail for six months. The strike collapsed.

The smashing of the ARU and his jail term turned Debs from a labor leader to a political radical. "The issue is Socialism versus Capitalism," he declared in 1897. "I am for Socialism because I am for humanity!" Millions of embittered workers followed him into the Socialist Party of America, and sought to elect him President. His vote soared from eighty-eight thousand in 1900 to almost nine hundred thousand by 1912. Establishment extremists kept a worried eye on his growing popularity.

Extremism was to be found as well among press tycoons who practiced "yellow journalism"—publishers like William Randolph Hearst (New York *Journal*) and Joseph Pulitzer (New York *World*). When insurrection broke out against Spanish rule in Cuba on February 24, 1895, both found that sensationalized atrocity stories about Spanish cruelty sold newspapers.

Hearst wrote of Spanish General Valeriano Weyler: "There is nothing to prevent his carnal, animal brain from running riot with itself in inventing tortures and infamies of bloody debauchery." He used the tales of Cuban exiles in the United States to whip up sentiment for American intervention, much as was done half a century later when Castro came to power in Cuba.

President William McKinley, no fool, resisted the pressure of the yellow journalists, announcing coldly that he would stand for "no jingo nonsense." But behind his back Theodore Roosevelt, now Assistant Secretary of the Navy, called the President "a white-livered cur" with "no more backbone than a chocolate eclair!" The jingos soon had their way.

On February 15, 1898, the USS *Maine* blew up in Havana Harbor, killing 260 officers and men. The Spanish insisted that the battleship's boilers had blown up; American naval officers blamed a mine; no responsible investigators blamed an intentional act by the Spanish government. But Hearst's *Journal* ran the headline: "DESTRUCTION OF THE WAR SHIP MAINE WAS THE WORK OF AN ENEMY. *Assistant Secretary Roosevelt Convinced the Explosion of the War Ship Was Not an Accident*". Public opinion, already inflamed by extremist reporting in the yellow press, picked up its war cry: "Remember the *Maine!*"

Madrid did everything possible to conciliate Washington, but Congress, the press, and nationalistic extremists like Roosevelt and Henry Cabot Lodge clamored for war. McKinley reluctantly gave in, leading Hearst to boast later, "How do you like the *Journal's* war?" In the grip of war fever, Americans sang

There'll Be A Hot Time In the Old Town Tonight and *The Stars and Stripes Forever.*

New fortunes were made by war profiteers out of spoiled food, inferior guns and ammunition, shoddy clothing, and defective medical supplies. Colonel Theodore Roosevelt of the Rough Riders dashed up San Juan hill to reach the Presidency of the United States as a hero of what Secretary of State John Hay fondly termed "a splendid little war." Spain was forced to cede to the United States victors the Philippines, Puerto Rico, and Guam, and to free Cuba into the American sphere of influence.

Angered by this triumph of the jingoists, Charles Francis Adams, William Graham Sumner, Carl Schurz, and other leading intellectuals met in Boston in November 1898, to form an Anti-Imperialist League. They denounced the acquisition of colonial possessions as a violation of American democracy by forcing millions of people to submit to foreign rule.

The issue was fought out in the election campaign of 1900, with Bryan leading the Democrats in opposing imperialism, and McKinley and Roosevelt defending the Spanish-American War and its colonial gains. The Republicans won.

McKinley's assassination in 1901 made Roosevelt President, and the "old Rough Rider" lost no time in demonstrating his conviction that the United States should "speak softly and carry a big stick." He was outraged when Colombia's legislators refused to sell the United States the right to build a canal across Panama, denouncing them as "foolish and homicidal corruptionists."

Arranging for a Panamanian junta to seize the land he wanted, he financed their uprising with $100,000 and sent three United States warships to protect them. Two hours after the junta declared Panama's "independence," Roosevelt recognized the new "government." Sixteen days later he had his treaty leasing the Canal Zone to the US "in perpetuity" for 40 million dollars.

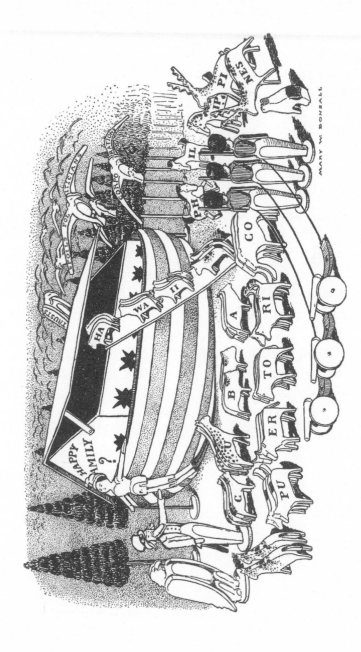

Father Noah: "Boys, if they don't come in quietly, bring on the cannon."

The "yellow journalists" were instrumental in stirring up American imperialism, "jingoism."

"I took the Canal Zone," he bragged eight years later, "and let Congress debate, and while the debate goes on, the canal does also." His extremism soured relations between the United States and Latin America for decades afterward, even though Wilson later offered Colombia an apology and indemnity.

Roosevelt did not stop with seizing Panama. In 1904 he announced a "Roosevelt corollary" to the Monroe Doctrine that flatly announced the United States would exercise "an international police power" whenever it felt the need to intervene in the internal affairs of other Western Hemisphere nations.

A few months later he sent troops into the Dominican Republic to control its finances. In the next two decades the power structure sent American troops to invade Haiti, Honduras, Nicaragua, Cuba, and other Central American republics.

Years later Marine General Smedley Butler, the much-decorated war hero who led many of these invasions, testified acidly before a Congressional committee, "I spent thirty-three years . . . being a high-class muscle man for Big Business, for Wall Street and the bankers." He did not admire Theodore Roosevelt.

12

Robber Barons, Wobblies, and Super-Patriots

Turn-of-the-century exposés of extremists in the power structure by journalists known as "muckrakers" shocked the nation. In *The Jungle,* Upton Sinclair spotlighted the processing of diseased meat by the Chicago packers. Its horrendous revelations turned many Americans vegetarian, creating an outcry for investigation of the industry. Edward Bok, in *The Ladies Home Journal,* exposed patent medicine manufacturers whose popular nostrums contained morphine and other dangerous drugs.

In *McClure's,* Ida Tarbell denounced the Standard Oil monopoly; Ray Stannard Baker reported the swindles of railroad tycoons; and Lincoln Steffens, in a series called *The Shame of the Cities,* revealed the links between big business and crooked politicians at every level of American government.

"Political corruption," Steffens concluded in 1906, was "a regularly established custom of the country, by which our political leaders . . . conduct the government of the city, State and Nation, not for the common good, but for the special interests of private business." He saw no sense in replacing "honest crooks" with reformers who often proved just as vulnerable to bribery. The fault, he insisted, lay with Americans who tolerated a corrupt political system that allowed big business to buy and control public officials. He told one reformer impatiently, "If you don't like the system, *change it*. If you refuse to change the system, then shut up!"

Steffens began as an earnest reformer, but ended as an avowed extremist. Losing faith in the ability of Americans to curb power structure extremists, he became a Communist sympathizer. After visiting the Soviet Union in 1919 with the official William C. Bullitt mission, and meeting Lenin, he wrote enthusiastically, "I have seen the future and it works!" He died in 1936, two decades before Khrushchev's denunciation of Stalin could shake his trust in the Soviet experiment.

Public support for the muckrakers compelled the government to begin alleged "trust-busting" actions against big business, investigations into political corruption, and legal action against the meat-packers, drug companies, and other exposed Establishment extremists. Sensitive to the prevailing political winds, President Theodore Roosevelt quickly attacked the trusts so vehemently that Establishment-controlled newspapers denounced him as a "trust-busting Socialist." The *New York Sun* forbade his name to be mentioned in its columns.

In reality, Roosevelt privately approved many of the trusts as practical. His carefully publicized gestures of breaking up Standard Oil and United States Steel left both monopolies untouched. It was even "trust-buster Teddy" who derisively labeled the journalistic crusaders against the corporations "muckrakers."

But his public image as a trust-buster won him another term in the 1904 elections. When he finally left the White House four years later, the trusts were stronger, if quieter in their operations, than when Roosevelt first became President.

The Establishment defeat of the Pullman strikers spurred a wave of excessive court decisions against labor unions. An Illinois law limiting the hours of labor for women in sweatshops was

"A nauseating job, but it must be done." President Theodore Roosevelt, pressured by the muckrakers, initiated government investigations of the meat-packing scandal.

invalidated because it "denied to women the same right of contract as men." The Supreme Court set aside a New York law limiting the workday of bakery employees for "depriving" them of their right to work longer. But courts upheld company injunctions against strikes; yellow-dog contracts that forbade workers to join unions; child labor; and the right of police to break up labor demonstrations and strikes.

A bitter reply came from the Wobblies—International Workers of the World (IWW). Their leader was anarchist Bill Haywood, who led the Western Federation of Miners in a violent struggle, between 1900 and 1905, that became known as the Rocky Mountain Revolution. When miners went out on strike in Montana, Idaho, and Colorado, clashes with mine guards, militia, and federal troops ended in the deaths, arrests, and deportation of miners.

Mines and smelters began blowing up in dynamite blasts. Mine officials, operators, strikebreakers, and innocent bystanders were killed in explosions. Arrested for murder, Wobblies insisted that the atrocities were the work of *agents provocateurs* hired by the corporations to frame them.

When Haywood and two other IWW leaders were arraigned for the dynamite death of Idaho's ex-Governor Frank Steunenberg, Socialist leader Eugene Debs roused the country to their defense as labor martyrs. President Roosevelt wrote a private letter that became public, intimating that they ought to be convicted, guilty or not, as "undesirable citizens." Debs distributed a million lapel buttons reading, "I Am An Undesirable Citizen," worn defiantly by labor sympathizers, all over the country.

Haywood and his co-defendants were acquitted after a brilliant trial defense by Clarence Darrow. Undaunted by the power structure, convinced he was in the vanguard of a workers' revolution, Haywood continued fomenting strikes by loggers, copper miners, migratory harvest hands, and Massachusetts textile workers getting ten dollars for a fifty-four-hour work week.

In 1916 the United States Commission on Industrial Relations reported to President Woodrow Wilson that the big corporations had created "social unrest and bitterness" by throwing against strikers not only municipal police, sheriffs, deputies, and militia, but also private guards, detectives, and vigilante organizations "which usurp and exercise the functions of the police." New York Police Commissioner Woods also testified that when he took office in 1913, he found the police under orders to suppress all radical street meetings, a policy provoking riots and widespread hostility toward law enforcement.

A new form of American extremism made itself felt when Russian pogroms in the 1880s and 1890s set off a wave of Jewish immigration to the United States. Like the Catholics before them, the Jews aroused a hostile reaction by "native Americans." Leading the anti-Semitic bigots was Thomas E. Watson of Georgia who, until 1913, had concentrated on attacking Catholics and blacks in his weekly paper, *The Jeffersonian,* and monthly *Watson's Magazine.* A former Populist candidate for President, Watson had grown rich investing in plantations worked by sharecroppers. Ambitious to become a Senator, he sought the support of half-literate rustics by appeals to prejudice.

His big opportunity came with the arrest of Leo Frank, a Jewish graduate of Cornell who was part-owner of a Marietta, Georgia, pencil factory, for the abuse and murder of fourteen-year-old Mary Phagan in the factory's cellar. Before she died she managed to scribble a note charging an unnamed black man with the crime. But Frank was indicted instead.

Georgia anti-Semites threatened court officials, "Hang the Jew, or we'll hang you!" Mobs gathered outside the courthouse, threatening to riot if Frank were not convicted. When he was sentenced to hang, the mobs celebrated jubilantly.

Leading papers throughout the country denounced the trial as a travesty of justice. Watson lashed back in his publications, accusing Frank and all Jews as "ritual murderers." When Governor John M. Slayton responded to national indignation by commuting Frank's sentence to life imprisonment, Watson denounced him as "King of the Jews and Traitors." Agitated by Watson's ravings an armed "vigilance committee" broke into the jail, seized Frank, and lynched him. "A Vigilance Committee redeems Georgia!" Watson's weekly crowed.

The *Chicago Tribune* called Georgia "a region of illiteracy, blatant self-righteousness and violence." *The Boston Traveler* said, "In this crowning demonstration of her inherent savagery, Georgia stands revealed before the world in her naked barbarian brutality." But Watson got what he was after—election to the United States Senate in 1920.

When he died two years later, Senator Harris, a fellow Georgian, declared, "He was always fighting for the masses of the people." Senator Trammel called him "a great and illustrious Georgian—a great American." Public funds paid for a 294-page government book carrying these and similar Congressional eulogies. None mentioned a word of Watson's long record as a notorious racial and religious bigot.

Early in 1914 the miners of Rockefeller-owned Colorado Fuel & Iron Company struck against intolerable working conditions. The company brought in three hundred strikebreakers as "deputy sheriffs," leading to inevitable clashes. Colorado's governor called out the National Guard. The jails were quickly filled with strikers, who were denied bail on grounds of "military necessity." Then militia raided the strikers' camp and set it afire, killing one strike leader and burning to death two women and eleven children.

This "Ludlow massacre" infuriated the striking miners, who swept through the region wrecking and burning mines and killing guards until federal troops were able to restore order.

The company's extremism brought a public outcry against absentee director John D. Rockefeller Jr., who actually had known nothing about the company's rabid labor policy. He was shocked to find himself being held accountable, and also blamed in the confusion for his father's old Standard Oil sins. It was then that Ivy Lee was called in to erase the stigma from the family name and give it a new public image.

The Ludlow massacre left its burning imprint on *that* Rockefeller's son Nelson over half a century later. As Governor of New York in 1968, he was asked by Mayor John Lindsay to call out the National Guard to clear garbage from the streets of New York City when the sanitation workers went out on strike in defiance of state law. Rockefeller refused, saying, "You can't move garbage with bayonets."

Unwilling to be blamed for another Ludlow massacre as his father had been, he offered the strikers a settlement instead and they went back to work. Lindsay bitterly assailed the move as a sacrifice of principle to expediency. Press denunciations also hurt Rockefeller's chances of being made the Republican candidate for President in 1968.

On May 7, 1915, when a German U-boat sank the *Lusitania*, killing 128 Americans aboard, ultra-patriots quickly mounted an extremist movement directed against those who opposed the United States' entry into the war. Two events in July 1916, triggered a wave of national hysteria. A bomb thrown into a San Francisco "preparedness" parade killed many marchers, bringing about a sentence of life imprisonment on flimsy evidence for two radical labor leaders, Thomas J. Mooney and Warren K. Billings. Eight days later a munitions explosion on

Black Tom Island, New Jersey, touched off a nationwide hunt for saboteurs.

When President Wilson took America into the war on April 6, 1917, opposition was silenced by the Espionage Act of June 15 and the Sedition Act a year later. Anyone uttering "disloyal or abusive" language about the government, the Constitution, the flag or the uniform, was punished by severe fines and jail terms, an ominous echo of the oppressive Alien and Sedition Acts engineered by John Adams.

Among the fifteen hundred Americans arrested for "disloyalty" were Socialists, Marxists, pacifists, anarchists, "hyphenated Americans" (German and Irish Americans who had no love for the British), and cynics who scorned the war as a struggle for commercial markets between English and German capitalists. Ironically, after the war Wilson admitted in a speech that the cynics' analysis of the war had been a correct one.

But ultra-patriots whipped up public passions against "atrocities of the Hun," support for the "noble aims of the Allies," and mob attacks against "pacifist traitors." George Creel, Chairman of the Administration's Committee of Public Information, admitted, "The press, from which we had the right to expect help, failed us miserably. . . . The chauvinists had the field to themselves, singing their hymns of hate."

Intolerance grew even worse following the outbreak of the Russian Revolution. Debs' Socialist Party was confused with the Communist Party. "Socialism," sneered the Detroit *Journal,* "is Bolshevism with a shave!"

In Canton, Ohio, on June 16, 1918, Debs publicly challenged the war extremists with his own anti-war extremism. Making a defiant speech as Socialist candidate for President, he declared, "I am opposed to every war but one . . . the world-wide war of social revolution." Promptly arrested, he was sentenced to ten years in jail and deprived of his citizenship.

"The court of final resort is the people," he said hopefully, "and that court will be heard from in due time." In 1920 he ran for President from jail and received almost 920,000 votes. Wilson, stung by Debs' opposition, refused to pardon him when the war was over. This act of grace had to come from an ultra-conservative, Republican President Warren Harding.

The war brought out an unexpected streak of extremism in one of America's most respected industrial geniuses—Henry Ford. On December 4, 1915, before America's involvement, he chartered a "peace ship" to sail for Norway on a zany mission "to get the boys out of the trenches by Christmas." Germany and the Allies both laughed at his naivete.

A postwar act of extremism by Ford was more serious. As owner-publisher of *The Dearborn Independent,* with a circulation of seven hundred thousand, he sought to blame the Jewish people for the war. He reprinted something called the "Protocols of the Elders of Zion" as "proof" of a Jewish conspiracy to control the world through crafty manipulation of Christian puppets.

What were the protocols? They were investigated in 1935 as part of a Swiss law case. The court found that they had originated in Russia in 1905 when the Tsar, frightened by an abortive revolution, was advised to divert the lightning of Russian discontent onto the Jews as a scapegoat. On orders, a Russian priest named Sergei Nilus "discovered" a faked document alleged to be a resolution by two dozen "Wise Men of Zion" for taking over the world. This forgery became the basis for a book by a Tsarist agent, *The Enemies of the Human Race.*

Appearing in 1906, it was widely reprinted all over Europe and Asia. And Ford, in November 1920, had revived the sham in his newspaper's series called "The International Jew." The Swiss court verdict fifteen years later ruled that the so-called documents on which it was based were "a forgery, a plagiarism, and silly nonsense."

Jewish Americans were outraged at Ford. In March 1927, when he introduced his new Model-A, they declared a boycott, supported by many sympathetic Catholics and Protestants. Ford was compelled to make a humiliating public apology.

"I confess I am deeply mortified," he wrote on July 7, 1927, "that this journal [*The Dearborn Independent*] . . . has been made the medium for resurrecting exploded fictions, for giving currency to the so-called protocols of the wise men of Zion which have been demonstrated, as I learn, to be gross forgeries." Jewish Americans welcomed this belated confession of extremism and called off the boycott.

But Ford's apology could not cancel the wide circulation given to the spurious protocols. In later years other anti-Semitic extremists—notably Father Charles Coughlin in the United States and Adolph Hitler in Germany—would find them useful.

The war also brought about the revival of another instrument of prejudice, the Ku Klux Klan. The new Klan was organized in Atlanta by Colonel William J. Simmons on November 25, 1915, although its members had not been idle during the previous quarter century. Between 1889 and 1918 a recorded total of 2,500 blacks were murdered—"on general principles," as H. L. Mencken once wrote sarcastically. But now the Klan extended its unique brand of Christianity to the North, where many blacks had jobs in war industries, as well.

The Klan helped inflame white bigotry against blacks. In 1917 a bloody riot in East St. Louis, Illinois, resulted in the death of forty-seven workers, almost all black. In July 1919, new race riots broke out in Chicago, New York, and Omaha.

Klan officials had a vested interest in prejudice, prospering on fat salaries and the sale of hooded gowns (600 percent profit) and other Klan paraphernalia. David Stephenson, Grand

Dragon of Indiana, was found to have made millions out of membership fees and nightshirts before he was arrested and convicted for murder.

At first the Wobblies openly branded World War I an imperialist struggle and exhorted, "Don't be a soldier—be a man!" Bill Haywood said, "All class-conscious IWW members are conscientiously opposed to spilling the life blood of human beings . . . because we believe that the interests and welfare of the working class in all countries are identical."

After America's entry into the war, he soft-pedaled the IWW's anti-militarism, aware that the power structure could smash the Wobblies with arrests for "disloyalty." But IWW-led strikes were still denounced by the press as "the work of Bolsheviki traitors." In July 1917, an IWW strike leader in Butte, Montana, was seized, beaten, dragged by rope behind a speeding car, then hanged from a railroad trestle.

Two months later Attorney General A. Mitchell Palmer sent a hundred federal agents to raid IWW branch headquarters in fifty cities, seizing their files. Three weeks later 166 IWW leaders were arrested and indicted in Chicago for violation of the Espionage Act. Palmer's raids continued until he had the entire leadership of the IWW behind bars.

This act of extremism followed discovery of an anarchistic or maniacal plot to assassinate thirty-six leading government officials and business tycoons. Packaged bombs deposited in the post office were addressed to Palmer himself, United States Postmaster General Albert Burleson, Supreme Court Justice Oliver Wendell Holmes, J. P. Morgan, John D. Rockefeller, and other notables.

Instead of conducting an efficient investigation, Palmer, who had Presidential ambitions, won dramatic headlines as a knight errant saving America from all radicals—Bolsheviks, Socialists,

Wobblies, aliens, labor leaders, and pacifists. Mass arrests followed a series of lawless raids on homes and labor headquarters. In January 1920, on one night, over four thousand persons were arrested on suspicion in thirty-three different cities. In Detroit three hundred men were arrested on false charges, held for a week in jail, denied food for twenty-four hours, then found innocent.

Extremists everywhere were quick to take their cue from Palmer. In West Virginia 150 alleged members of the IWW were seized, forced to kiss the flag, then deported. In Lynn, Massachusetts, thirty-nine people were put behind bars for gathering to discuss formation of a cooperative. Mobs tarred, feathered, and lynched labor leaders who spoke with a German accent.

As a crowning touch, the New York State Legislature expelled five legally elected members of the Socialist Party from its Assembly, to the indignation of Supreme Court Justice Charles Evans Hughes.

Ultra-patriotic groups denounced labor leaders and intellectuals as Bolsheviks who should be jailed or deported. The Allied Patriotic Societies gravely assured New York Governor Al Smith that the Reds were holding ten thousand meetings a week in the nation. In 1921 Vice President Calvin Coolidge castigated America's universities as hotbeds of sedition.

The Palmer raids drove the small handful of real Communists underground. In 1921 they emerged under a new name—the Workers Party of America, led by William Z. Foster. "They believed in violent revolution and said so," J. Edgar Hoover noted. Although their membership was little more than twelve thousand, Foster declared, "We no longer measure the importance of revolutionary organizations by size. In some places where there are only one or two men, more results are obtained than where they have larger organizations."

The militancy of these extremists disturbed both Socialists and labor leaders whose primary concern was decent wages and hours for workers. In the 1919 steel strike Communists angered union leaders by exhorting strikers over their heads.

13

Jazz Age and Depression Extremists

In 1918 America's allies, Britain and France, sought to crush the Bolshevik threat posed by Lenin's seizure of power in Russia. Arming and supplying a counter-revolutionary White Russian army, they sent a supporting Allied Expeditionary Force to Siberia and demanded ten thousand American troops to rescue Czech forces trapped in Siberia by Russia's withdrawal from the war.

When Wilson agreed, they cynically used the Americans in clashes with the Red Army, thus violating the President's own Fourteen Points promising self-determination for all nations. The Russians never forgot this United States involvement in an extremist military adventure to overthrow their government, remaining constantly suspicious of the United States' intentions.

Wilson made other serious mistakes on the heels of victory. In the 1918 Congressional elections, he appealed for a Democratic victory as a vote of confidence in his leadership, even though the Republicans had co-operated in a bipartisan war effort. But the American people, tired of war and Wilson, gave the Republicans a big majority in both Houses. "THE WORKERS MUST CAPTURE THE POWER OF THE STATE! THEY MUST WREST

FROM THE CAPITALISTS THE MEANS THROUGH WHICH THE
CAPITALIST RULE IS MAINTAINED. The answer to the Dictatorship of the Capitalists is the Dictatorship of the Workers."

Such extremism was exploited by the companies to smear the
strike as Communist-inspired, alienating public support. As one
disgruntled labor leader said in disgust, "With friends like the
Communists, who needs enemies?"

Stung, Wilson compounded his mistake by going to the
Paris Peace Conference personally without a single important
Republican consultant. Republican leaders promptly warned the
British and French to pay no attention to Wilson's demands for
a League of Nations to safeguard the peace, since he had been
discredited by the 1918 elections.

Senator Henry Cabot Lodge, who hated Wilson and now
dominated the Senate, was every inch as rigid in his views and
policies as Wilson. He made the question of the League a personal vendetta between himself and the President. The Senate rejected the Versailles Treaty and America failed to join
the League—a tragedy of extremism which ultimately led
to the weak League's downfall and the rise of Mussolini and
Hitler.

Disillusionment over the war and Versailles turned most Americans against any further involvement with European powers.
During the war the National Security League, lobbying for
big armaments appropriations, had urged, "Help save America!
America is in danger of losing her soul."

In 1919 a Congressional investigation found that the league's
backers were well-known "merchants of death" who combined
ultrapatriotism and profits. House of Representatives Report
Number n73 said, "If the curtain were only pulled back . . . the
hands of Rockefeller, of Vanderbilt, of Morgan, of Remington,

of duPont, and of Guggenheim, would be seen, suggesting steel, oil, moneybags . . . rifles, powder and railroads."

Other exposés showed arms manufacturers selling their wares impartially to both sides, making fortunes out of mass killing. The public also saw grim photos, previously censored, of pitifully mutilated American war casualties. Anti-war books, plays, and movies like John Dos Passos's *Three Soldiers,* Ernest Hemingway's *A Farewell to Arms,* and Erich Maria Remarque's *All Quiet On the Western Front,* portrayed war as a senseless horror.

Public sentiment swung away from the extreme of war hysteria to the opposite extreme of cynical isolationism. Americans wanted nothing more to do with the world beyond the oceans, its problems, its League of Nations, its interminable wars.

They sought instead a long-delayed, desperate gaiety and irresponsibility that made the twenties "the jazz age." At the most extreme fringe were the Bohemians, who were that generation's dropouts from society, like our beatniks and hippies. The Bohemian capital was Greenwich Village in New York City, where they sought to create a community that emphasized individuality, eccentricity, self-expression, paganism, anti-respectability, female equality, and impulsive living.

"My candle burns at both ends; It will not last the night;" wrote Edna St. Vincent Millay, high priestess of the Bohemians. "But ah, my foes, and oh, my friends—It gives a lovely light!" When the Village became overcrowded with pseudo-Bohemians and Bohemian-watchers, many artists, writers and musicians fled to Paris, where they spent most of the twenties as "the lost generation" of expatriates.

Made famous in novelist F. Scott Fitzgerald's *This Side of Paradise,* the Bohemians set the styles for the period—bobbed hair, short skirts, smoking and drinking for women, casual moral standards, divorce, the Charleston, and the shimmy. Their revolt collapsed with the depression of 1929.

The churches of the twenties, incensed by the jazz age, were in no mood to tolerate a further breakdown of religious influence by the spread of scientific education. In the South particularly, the Darwinian theory of evolution was held to be blasphemous. Extremist church pressure even made it illegal to teach evolution in certain states. John Scopes, a Tennessee schoolteacher, was arrested in 1925 for violating this law.

Prosecuting him for the state, William Jennings Bryan based his argument on the incontestability of the Book of Genesis, while Clarence Darrow defended Scopes and the accuracy of the Darwin theory. Following their great courtroom debate, it was nationally agreed that Darrow had easily won the case for Darwin; but he had lost it for Scopes, who was found guilty of violating Tennessee law, as charged, and fined a hundred dollars, a fine later set aside on appeal.

Two other extremist forces had already won victories at law. The Women's Rights movement had achieved the Nineteenth Amendment to the Constitution, giving women the vote; and Prohibitionists had won the Eighteenth Amendment, outlawing alcoholic beverages. The Volstead Act of 1919 also empowered the federal government to enforce prohibition, a drastic law which promptly provoked widespread defiance.

The nation was plunged into a lawless era as racketeers like Al Capone, Legs Diamond, and Dutch Schultz fought bloody gang wars to monopolize the bootlegging trade. Americans by the millions broke the law by drinking bootleg whiskey or gin— much of it poisonous wood alcohol that killed or blinded those who drank it.

The speakeasies were supplied by secret stills whose canvas-covered trucks were often hijacked by rival bootleggers, and by rumrunners who dodged the Coast Guard to bring liquor car-goes from Cuba or seaport stills. In four years Chicago had 215 unsolved gang murders. The Chicago chief of police admitted that "fifty percent of Chicago's police force are identified with the bootlegging industry."

What had begun as an extremist "noble experiment" ended in dismal failure. By 1928 the nation began to divide politically into "wets" and "drys," with the Democrats nominating New York's Governor Al Smith, who proposed ending prohibition and returning the alcohol problem to the states, and the Republicans backing "dry" candidate Herbert Hoover.

Smith lost, less because he was a "wet" than because he was a Catholic. The inevitable hate propaganda against "rum, Romanism and rebellion" was intensified to defeat him so badly—by over a six million vote margin—that no Catholic candidate was nominated for President by the Democrats until John F. Kennedy in 1960. But prohibition was finally dumped in February 1933, by the Twenty-first Amendment that was passed at the outset of Franklin D. Roosevelt's administration.

When the stock market crashed on October 29, 1929, the nation began sliding headlong into a disastrous depression, with unemployment reaching fifteen million by the end of 1932. Hoover's failure to offer government remedies during those three years alienated Americans as a form of free enterprise extremism. "Any lack of confidence in . . . the basic strength of business . . . is foolish," he insisted.

When public pressure forced the House to introduce a bill appropriating two billion dollars for public works, he said, "This is not unemployment relief. It is the most gigantic pork barrel ever perpetrated by the American Congress." He waited until the Presidential election year of 1932 before creating the Reconstruction Finance Corporation (RFC) to lend money to industry, railroads, banks, and agricultural agencies to get the sick economy back on its feet. It was too little too late.

The depression and national discontent spurred the radical Left into action. An American Communist delegation in Moscow heard Joseph Stalin tell them, "I think the moment is not far off when a revolutionary crisis will develop in America. . . . It is essential that the American Communist Party should be capable of meeting that historical moment."

The first step, Stalin said, was to purge the party of followers of Leon Trotsky, the rival he had defeated in a Russian struggle for power during 1928–29. So the American Communist Party expelled its Trotskyite faction, which organized into a new extremist wing, the Socialist Workers Party, under Jay Lovestone and Benjamin Gitlow.

The purge of the Communist Party by its leaders, William Z. Foster and Earl Browder, reduced their ranks to only 7,500 members in 1930. But four years later they had thirty thousand followers. The CP's real strength was in the leadership it planted through Red "cells" in industrial plants, trade unions, youth organizations, antiwar, and anti-Fascist leagues that sprang up during the thirties.

The Communists were always the hardest-working members of progressive organizations, often winning key posts and great influence by their willingness to sacrifice all their time and effort for the organization cause. But they were never independent. When the party line conflicted with the best interests of the cause, they followed the party line, sincerely convinced that Moscow always knew best.

With thousands of firms bankrupt, factories closed, long bread lines in the cities, and college men selling apples on streetcorners, jobless veterans decided, in desperation, to revive the extremist tactic of Coxey's Army. A "Bonus Army" of twenty thousand descended on Washington to compel Congress to vote military bonuses that had been promised to World War I veterans.

In June 1932, veterans set up camp with their wives and children in lean-tos, shanties, and tents on Anacostia Flats, determined to squat in the nation's capital until Congress passed the Bonus Bill. Their audacity angered President Hoover into an act of counter-extremism. General Douglas MacArthur was ordered to drive them out of their encampments. Leading troops down Pennsylvania Avenue, with a young major named Eisenhower behind him, he was met by boos and bricks.

The soldiers used tear gas to disperse the mob, and many spectators were injured in the wild stampede. The troops burned down the shacktowns, and MacArthur provided gas and oil for the cars of the dispossessed veterans, to enable them to get their families home. The next day the nation's press accused both Hoover and MacArthur of callous brutality toward jobless veterans who had once been hailed as patriotic heroes.

The drastic Bonus Army affair did much to turn angry Americans against Herbert Hoover in the 1932 elections.

In so pronounced a climate of discontent, the election of the Democratic candidate who promised the American people a New Deal was almost inevitable. Roosevelt won a landslide victory—22,823,000 votes to Hoover's 15,762,000.

Even though the country had never been more ripe for extremist solutions to its problems, Norman Thomas won only 882,000 votes for the Socialists; William Z. Foster only 103,000 for the Communists; the Trotskyites (Socialist Labor) only 33,000; Prohibitionists, 82,000; and old Jacob Coxey of Coxey's Army fame won only 7,300 for a Farmer Labor ticket.

It was obvious that the American people distrusted the extremists, preferring to pin their faith on the more liberal of the two major political parties. Extremist candidates charged that this was inevitable as long as the major parties had millions of dollars for campaigning and propaganda, controlling between them the lion's share of space in news media.

Most members of the power structure favored Hoover, although a few like Hearst, whose papers glorified Fascist Italy, saw Roosevelt as a potential American Mussolini. "Any man who has the brains to think and the nerve to act for the benefit of the people of the country," he declared on October 24, 1932, "is considered a radical by those who are content with stagnation and willing to endure disaster." But his support of F.D.R. was short-lived, and he soon joined the chorus of Establishment hate against the new President.

Roosevelt, a shrewd and intelligent member of the power structure, was not an extremist but a reformer, convinced that the only way to save capitalism was to correct its excesses. Big business extremists, he felt, would provoke revolution if they persisted in the rigid policies that had brought the country to the edge of chaos under Hoover.

He sought to restore the prestige of the free enterprise system with his New Deal program for the "forgotten man." A flood of new legislation poured through Congress, giving the government control of the nation's economic affairs. Bank panics were stopped by deposit insurance; needy families received federal relief aid; work was made for the jobless.

The Works Project Administration (WPA) created employment at the same time it provided the nation with rural electrification, reforestation, federal theaters, flood control, state guidebooks, slum clearance, new parks, schools, and airports. Even Republican Governor Alf Landon of Kansas, Roosevelt's Presidential rival in 1936, felt compelled to write to him in 1934, "This civil works program is one of the soundest, most constructive policies of your administration."

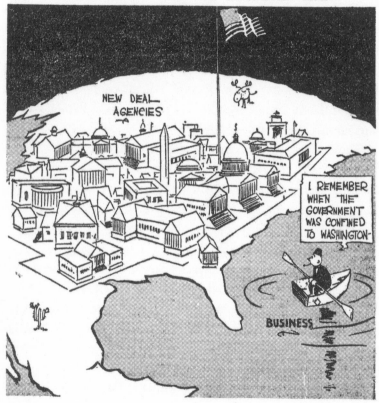

Cartoonist Borgstedt presents one view of the growth of federal agencies under the New Deal.

But demagogues of right, left, and center kept urging the American people to support their own extremist programs.

In 1932 a new movement called Technocracy advocated turning the economy over to professionally trained engineers, who possessed the scientific know-how to reshape it technically and make it work properly.

In 1934 Dr. Francis E. Townsend of California won followers for his Townsend Plan to end the depression by paying every American over sixty the sum of two hundred dollars a month to be spent the same month, thus providing a business stimulus.

That same year Senator Huey "Kingfish" Long of Louisiana unveiled his "Share the Wealth" program ("Every man a King!"). He promised every American a $6,000 homestead allowance, a $2,500 income, a car, and a radio. He also reorganized the Louisiana state government to make it a personal dictatorship.

"Of course we can have Fascism in this country," he said, "but we'll have to call it anti-Fascism." Political commentator Raymond Gram Swing acknowledged that he had made some liberal reforms as Louisiana's governor, but said, "His movement, in a crude way, was designed to win national power by the same appeal as that of the Italian fascists and the German Nazis. . . . He wanted to do good because he knew it was the way to achieve power." General Hugh S. Johnson, director of the New Deal's National Recovery Act (NRA) program, said bluntly, "Adolf Hitler has nothing on him!"

It was later learned that Long had planned with Dr. Townsend and Father Charles Coughlin, another extremist, to head a Union Party ticket in the 1936 Presidential elections. But Long's aspirations died with his assassination at the hands of a crazed man whose family he had allegedly ruined.

Upton Sinclair, elderly muckraking author of *The Jungle*, ran unsuccessfully for Governor of California on the Democratic ticket advocating an extremist plan called EPIC—End Poverty

In California. Similar to the Townsend idea, EPIC proposed to end poverty by high income and inheritance taxes to provide pensions for all over sixty. Sinclair also proposed reorganizing American society into cooperative Utopias like those of the nineteenth century, which had failed so dismally.

Perhaps the most influential extremist of the period was Father Charles Coughlin, the anti-Semitic "radio priest" of Detroit, who headed the National Union for Social Justice. He blasted the New Deal as the "Jew Deal," and called President Roosevelt a liar, although he subsequently apologized.

He referred to the discredited *Protocols of Zion* to slander Jews; explained Communism as "an international Jewish conspiracy"; and parroted the Nazi line in his broadcasts and weekly *Social Justice*. Collaborating with other pro-Fascist extremists, he helped organize the Christian Front, an allegedly anti-Communist, but basically anti-Semitic, movement.

Christian Front speakers demanded that "Jewish blood flow all over America," and that "every Jew in the United States must hang." In 1939 New York City's Mayor Fiorello La Guardia ordered 233 Christian Fronters arrested for inciting to riot. But by 1940 they claimed a membership of three hundred thousand many organized as storm troopers to break up any meeting they disliked.

As Coughlin's links to the American Fascist movement and German Nazism became unmistakable, the Post Office barred his propaganda from the mails under the Espionage Act. Coughlin himself was finally ordered by the Catholic Archdiocese of Detroit to stop his extremist propaganda.

Another assault on the New Deal came from anti-Roosevelt big business leaders who organized the American Liberty League in 1934. It helped finance radical Right movements like the Sentinels of the Republic, the Southern Committee to Uphold the Constitution and the Tool Owners Union, which was denied a corporate charter by New York State for being fascist.

The United Press ran a headline: "LIBERTY LEAGUE CON-TROLLED BY OWNERS OF $37,000,000." Senator Robert M. LaFollette Jr., noting that the biggest League contributions came from some of the wealthiest men in America, said, "It is not an organization that can be expected to defend the liberty of the masses of the American people. It speaks for the vested interests." The League attacked Roosevelt as a power-mad dictator out to destroy the free enterprise system, and saw the Wagner National Labor Relations Act as a Red plot.

Testimony before the National Labor Relations Board (NLRB) revealed that the corporations were spending eighty million dollars a year on labor spies, scabs, tear gas, and machine guns.

In the same year that the Liberty League was organized, a fantastic radical Right plot was hatched to condemn the New Deal as Communist, then seize Washington in a military *putsch* and establish a Mussolini-style dictatorship under the guise of "a hundred percent Americanism." The man the well-heeled plotters selected to lead their march on Washington was popular United States Marine General Smedley Butler, twice winner of the Congressional Medal of Honor.

But to their dismay, General Butler, a loyal and intelligent American, exposed the plot to the McCormack-Dickstein Committee of the House of Representatives on December 29, 1934. Very soon after his testimony, the Liberty League made a sudden decision to disband their organization.

14

Hitlerites and Stalinites

In the 1936 elections the radical Right mustered anti-Roosevelt forces behind a Union Party led by Congressman William Lemke of North Dakota, who called F.D.R. a revolutionist. The President easily won re-election with almost 28 million votes, but Lemke received 882,000 ballots, far more than Norman Thomas on the Socialist ticket (187,000) and Communist Earl Browder (80,000). It was clear that the radical Right was becoming the strongest extremist force in America.

The radical Left grew increasingly disenchanted with Roosevelt and the New Deal, which they began decrying as "the death rattle of capitalism." Preparing for the class struggle for power they foresaw, they infiltrated labor unions, the National black Congress, the American Student Union, and the American Youth Congress. A few fanatical party members engaged in espionage for the Soviet Union, like federal employee Whittaker Chambers, who later turned informer.

Communists supported and were active in the Congress of Industrial Organizations (CIO), formed when John L. Lewis, dynamic leader of the United Mine Workers, led ten unions out of the AFL. The CIO "organized the unorganized" with a great wave of sit-down strikes in auto, steel, and other industries during 1936–37. Workers barricaded themselves in their factories night and day until the companies agreed to recognize and bargain with their unions. By the summer of 1937 the CIO's extremist tactics had won them four million members.

Big business fought back even more extremely. On May 30, 1937, one Chicago plant's company police opened machine gun fire on CIO demonstrators outside the plant, killing ten. Henry Ford, swearing he would shut down operations before dealing with a union, sanctioned terrorist methods in fighting his auto workers. His extremism so alienated his wife and son Edsel that they stopped speaking to him.

Blaming labor's militancy on Roosevelt, industrialists viewed him as a "traitor to his class," an aristocrat who had sold out to labor, liberals and leftists. They financed hate propaganda calling him "that cripple in the White House," "a Jew whose real name is Rosenfeld," "Franklin Double-Crosser Roosevelt." The President's wife Eleanor was slandered as a "card-carrying member of the Communist Party."

One Fort Worth oilman offered a pair of gorillas to the local zoo provided they be called Franklin and Eleanor. On the day the President died, a San Antonio millionaire threw a cocktail party to celebrate the "glad news."

During the thirties the thrust of Hitler and Mussolini to spread Fascism across the world, under a cloak of anti-Communism, polarized sympathies in America between anti-Fascists and isolationists who wanted no more involvement in European wars. United States Communists sought to manipulate anti-Fascists for pro-Soviet purposes in a "United Front."

United States rightists sought to capture the isolationist movement for pro-Fascist objectives in the America First Committee. Their hero was Charles Lindbergh, "the lone eagle" who had won world acclaim in 1927 for making the world's first solo flight across the Atlantic. Visiting Berlin in 1938, he was greatly impressed with German air power.

Accepting a high Nazi decoration from Field Marshal Herman Goring, he returned to predict defeat for the British, whom he denounced for having "encouraged the smaller nations of Europe to fight against hopeless odds." At an America First rally at Des Moines, Iowa, on September 11, 1941, he charged Jewish, British, and New Deal groups with attempting to force America into the war against Germany.

Christian Fronters and German American Bundists attacked peaceful anti-Fascist meetings shouting, "We want Hitler! We want Lindbergh!" President Roosevelt branded Lindbergh publicly as a defeatist and Nazi appeaser. Resigning his commission in the Air Reserve, Lindbergh retreated into seclusion. His former popularity faded rapidly, especially after Pearl Harbor united Americans against world Fascism.

The Bulletin of the Institute for Propaganda Analysis for January 1939, reported at least eight hundred pro-Fascist organizations in the United States. Fritz Kuhn marched brown-shirt troops of the German American Bund around Yorkville in New York, hailing the Swastika flag with Nazi salutes. William Dudley Pelley, uniformed leader of the Silver Shirt Legion of America, refused to stop disseminating Nazi propaganda after Pearl Harbor, and was sentenced to jail for fifteen years.

The Reverend Gerald B. Winrod of Wichita, Kansas, who claimed a hundred thousand followers for his Defenders of the Christian Faith, quoted the *Protocols of Zion* and praised Hitler as a German saint who had purified a Germany "defiled by Jewish immorality." He labeled the Catholic Church "the harlot of the Bible," reviving all the old Know-Nothing bigotry. The Federal Council of Churches, he wrote, was "Protestant papacy," and the NAACP was "a black nest of Reds."

In 1938 Winrod sought the Republican nomination for Senator. William Allen White, respected editor of the *Emporia Gazette,* warned fellow Kansans, "To nominate him, we must defend his position as a peddler of racial and religious hatred—a Nazi position." Winrod lost in the primary.

Most right wingers in the power structure preferred to keep aloof from the disreputable "lunatic fringe." They supported more respectable organizations like the National Economic Council led by Merwin K. Hart, leading apologist for General Francisco Franco's Spain. Hart opposed the Wagner Act, health insurance for employees, the right of citizens on relief to vote, and child labor laws (youth control).

"Merwin K. Hart . . . is well-known," said United States Supreme Court Justice Robert Jackson, "for his pro-Fascist leanings."

On the left, meanwhile, the Communist Party "bored from within" trade unions, student organizations, and anti-Fascist movements. They recruited new party members among liberals who were persuaded that the Communists sought the same goals they did—to defend democracy, civil rights, and trade unions from the radical Right—only more dynamically.

The United Front of liberals and Communists broke sharply with the Roosevelt administration for failing to aid Loyalist Spain against Franco's Fascist army, which was crushing Spanish democracy with help from Hitler and Mussolini.

But the United Front split wide open on August 23, 1939, when Joseph Stalin, fearful of Hitler's intentions, signed a non-aggression pact with him. Almost overnight the Communist Parties of the world followed the new Moscow line. Denunciations of Nazi Germany stopped, replaced by attacks on the British-French "imperialist warmongers," and on Roosevelt for supporting them. This surprise flip flop was too much for liberals and intellectuals involved in the struggle against Fascism.

Many unions expelled their Communists. There were wholesale defections from the Communist Party, whose prestige sank even lower when Stalin invaded Poland in September and Finland in November. The United Front collapsed.

Radical Left and radical Right, strange new bedfellows, jointly attacked Roosevelt as a warmonger for proposing, in January 1941, the Lend-Lease Act to help the Allies. Isolationist Senator Burton K. Wheeler paraphrased the New Deal program of crop control by warning that the ultimate result of the act would be to "plow under every fourth American boy."

The fortunes of war restored the world's Communist Parties to respectability. Hitler's doublecross of Stalin by his attack on Russia on June 22, 1941, made the Soviet Union the ally of England and France. It became America's ally, too, after Pearl Harbor. United States Communists worked and fought zealously for the war effort. Dismayed by the turn of events, the radical Right retreated into glum silence.

One Max Stephan of Detroit aided a Nazi flier to escape from a prison camp, becoming the first American to be sentenced to death for treason since the Whisky Rebellion. He boasted that Hitler would conquer the United States in time to free him. His reprieve came instead from President Roosevelt, who commuted his sentence to life imprisonment.

During 1944 the radical Right became vocal again in support of a "beat Japan first" movement, designed to ease the pressure on a losing Germany and bolster the prestige of General Douglas MacArthur, a right-wing idol. The Asian "yellow peril" was a favorite theme of the radical Right; almost immediately after the war they urged attacks on Red China.

A problem of power structure extremism arose at the close of the war over the use of America's first atomic or A-bombs. Should they be dropped first in a demonstration warning, to give Japan a chance to surrender without an unnecessary holocaust, or should they be dropped on one or two Japanese cities to terrify the enemy into immediate surrender? In the secret debate among President Harry S. Truman's advisers, some urged its use as a combat weapon to gain political advantages over the Soviet Union in postwar peace negotiations.

The extremists had their way. The first A-bomb, dropped on Hiroshima on August 6, 1945, burned four square miles to the ground, killing over sixty thousand men, women, and children. A second A-bomb exploded three days later over Nagasaki, killing thirty-six thousand more. Ever since, critics have denounced the bombings as needless atrocities against a defeated people on the verge of surrender. Truman's defenders insist that without them, it would have been necessary to lose over a million lives invading Japan itself to force an end to the war.

A postwar problem of power structure extremism confronted the Allies in the Nuremberg Trials of twenty-four Nazi leaders as war criminals. Right-wing sympathizers called the trials illegal because defendants were being prosecuted for "crimes against humanity," which had not been outlawed at the time they were committed. But half the defendants were hanged; seven received prison sentences; four were acquitted.

The trials established the principle that no government official or member of the armed forces could plead "orders" as an excuse for committing atrocities his conscience ought to tell him were "crimes against humanity." This Nuremberg principle was raised in the 1960s by Americans refusing to be drafted to fight in Vietnam, a war they saw as unjust.

Almost as soon as World War II was over, extremists of left and right began to advocate opposite courses for American foreign policy. The left demanded continued cooperation with the Soviet Union. The right urged anti-Communist moves in Europe and the Far East. Conflicting United States and Soviet interests in Europe, clashing in Germany, brought about the onset of the

Cold War. The American left, accusing Truman of risking a nuclear holocaust in an arms race against Stalin, led "Ban the Bomb" and "Better Red Than Dead" demonstrations.

The radical Right, complaining that Truman was "soft on Communism," mounted militant campaigns against Communism at home and abroad. Spearhead of their movement was the House Un-American Activities Committee which, in 1947, began hearings announced as intending to ferret out Communists in government, Hollywood, radio, and the universities.

Liberals who had in any way cooperated with Communists during the United Front years were smeared as "Commies" or "fellow travelers." Two radical Right publications, *Counterattack* and *Red Channels,* published their names in blacklists used to get them fired and to bar them from jobs. "Blacklisting," said playwright Elmer Rice, "is an ugly blot upon American life and an ugly threat to American liberty." Open blacklisting stopped when some noted liberals, outraged at being libeled as Reds, filed lawsuits and won heavy damages.

Seeking re-election in 1948, Truman was handicapped by desertions from the Democratic Party of both right and left extremist wings. States Rights Democrats (Dixiecrats), a rightist faction opposed to civil rights, nominated Governor Strom Thurmond of South Carolina. The new Progressive Party, opposed to Truman's Cold War policies, nominated former Vice President Henry Wallace. Nevertheless Truman upset the political polls by winning re-election over Republican Thomas E. Dewey with 24,100,000 votes. The Dixiecrats polled 1,169,000, an almost even heat with the Progressives' 1,158,000.

The Cold War and fears inspired by the United States-Union of Soviet Socialist Republics atomic arms race led to over sixteen thousand observation posts set up on rooftops, balconies, towers and mountaintops in 1949. For nine years 280,000 civilian volunteers manned them at a government cost of eight million dollars a' year, until President Dwight D. Eisenhower quietly abolished the operation in 1958. "There had been no public protest," said Professor Oliver C. Cox of Lincoln University, Missouri, "against the almost ridiculous propaganda about . . . the desperate need for naked-eye observation."

Following the defeat of Chiang Kai-shek by Mao Tse-tung, the Chinese Nationalists on Formosa set up a powerful lobby in Washington, paid for by United States aid funds. General Joseph Stilwell, describing his experiences in China during World War II, had revealed in his autobiography that Chiang had lost China because of his inept and corrupt regime. A United States White Paper on August 5, 1949, confirmed this. But the China Lobby, working with the radical Right, blamed Red China's victory on a conspiracy by "State Department traitors."

Primarily, they meant General George Marshall.

Radical Right agitation drove the Truman administration to appease its attackers by prosecuting the radical Left. On October 14, 1949, eleven Communist Party leaders were jailed for conspiracy to overthrow the government. The House Un-American Activities Committee began a spy hunt. Alger Hiss, a State Department official, was accused of being a Communist; he was sentenced to five years in jail for perjury.

Senator Joseph R. McCarthy of Wisconsin became the leading spokesman for the radical Right with a crusade against "Communists in government." Labeling key figures of the Roosevelt and Truman administrations as "Red traitors," he charged the Democrats with "twenty years of treason." His favorite gambit was holding up a piece of paper with lists which no one ever saw and telling an audience, "I have here a list of 205 names made known to the Secretary of State as members of the Communist Party, who are nevertheless still shaping policy in the

State Department." Sometimes he said the number was fifty-seven or eighty-one.

A Senate subcommittee under Democratic Senator Millard Tydings of Maryland investigated McCarthy's secret "evidence." His charges, Tydings reported, were "a fraud and a hoax." McCarthy lashed back by causing Tydings's defeat for re-election. He flooded Maryland with malicious propaganda that used faked photos to Red-bait and smear Tydings.

McCarthy made new headlines by demanding the impeachment of President Truman, and the firing of Secretary of State Dean Acheson. He branded General Marshall "a man steeped in falsehood . . . part of a conspiracy . . . always and invariably serving the Kremlin." Marshall was the man whom President Eisenhower later praised as the greatest living American.

McCarthy was clearly following Hitler's advice in *Mein Kampf:* "The size of the lie is a definite factor in causing it to be believed, for the vast masses of a nation are . . . easily deceived. . . . The primitive simplicity of their minds renders them a more easy prey to a big lie than a small one."

At the height of his four-year inquisition, a Gallup Poll survey revealed that the majority of Americans believed McCarthy's charges of guilt by association, guilt by collaboration, guilty by identification, and guilt by denunciation.

Likewise, when President Truman removed General MacArthur from command in Korea for insubordination, radical Right propaganda was so effective that the Gallup Poll showed only 29 percent of Americans supporting the President. McCarthy hailed MacArthur as a great general who had been deliberately stopped from winning the Korean War by White House treason.

"In making a political career of mud-slinging and Red-baiting," commented the *New York Times,* "Senator McCarthy has launched irresponsible, unprovable, and ridiculous charges

'HE BEEN CLEARED?'

Culver Pictures, Inc.
Senator Joseph McCarthy's anti-Communist drive brought a great many important people under suspicion.

against so many respected citizens that his attacks have become almost an accolade." Senator William Benton of Connecticut denounced McCarthy as unfit to hold office. McCarthyites fought Benton's re-election in 1952 and defeated him.

Winning his own re-election, McCarthy became chairman of the Senate Committee on Government Operations, as well as of its Permanent Subcommittee on Investigations, in a new Republican administration under President Eisenhower. He lost no time in making his new power felt. Over seven thousand federal employees were fired as "security risks" by government officials who were anxious to appease him. Fear of him grew steadily.

Attacking "Communism" in the academic world, he accused Harvard and Yale of being "sanctuaries" for Red professors. College faculties became afraid to discuss economics, government, modern history, or political economy in class. Their students became known as "the silent generation" out of fear of expressing opinions which might injure their careers.

Local extremists of the radical Right conducted heresy hunts to censor school textbooks. One member of the Indiana State Textbook Commission seriously charged, "There is a Communist directive in education now to stress the story of Robin Hood . . . because he robbed the rich and gave to the poor."

McCarthy accused the State Department's Information Service overseas libraries of having some left-wing authors on their shelves. Secretary of State John Foster Dulles hastily reported that the eleven books he had complained of had actually been burned. President Eisenhower grimly denounced book-burning in a speech at Dartmouth. But even he seemed immobilized by McCarthy's swashbuckling reign of terror.

"I just will not—I *refuse*—to get into the gutter with that guy!" he said in disgust. He waited for the American public to perceive McCarthy as a dangerous demagogue reaching for power on a ladder of defamation and distortion.

McCarthy finally overreached himself by opening hearings on "Communism in the Army." Subpoenaing Brigadier General Ralph Zwicker, one of the heroes of the Battle of the Bulge, he roared at him, "You are a disgrace to the uniform. You're shielding Communist conspirators. You're not fit to be an officer. You're ignorant. You are going to be put on public display." President Eisenhower, outraged, threw his support firmly behind the Armed Forces.

The resulting clash was the sensational Army-McCarthy hearings of the summer, 1954, televised to twenty million fascinated Americans. McCarthy was delighted with this chance to star as inquisitor before so vast an audience. He believed that Americans, who had never really been able to see him in action before, would be delighted by his extremist tactics.

It was a fatal miscalculation.

15

McCarthyism Falls; Birchism Rises

Americans were stunned by the spectacle of McCarthy sneering at and bullying witnesses, many clearly innocent of the outrageous charges he flung at them. Millions of former supporters grew ashamed of their mistake; other millions grew bored with his absurd grandstanding. The denouement came when he attempted to Red-bait an assistant to Joseph Welch, the gentle-spoken counsel representing the United States Army.

Welch, horrified, declared before twenty million Americans, "Until this moment, Senator, I think I had never gauged your cruelty or your recklessness. . . . Have you no sense of decency, sir? At long last? *Have you left no sense of decency?*"

Welch's indignation destroyed Joseph McCarthy. When the Wisconsin Senator left the hearing that day, other Senators turned their backs on him. "What did I do?" he asked in bewilderment, spreading his hands. He had only been as unethical as usual. But the public had finally seen his demagoguery through Welch's prism of outrage, and were revolted.

His downfall was swift. On July 30, 1954, Ralph Flanders of Vermont introduced a resolution of censure against him in the Senate. Alarmed, his Far Right supporters held a McCarthy rally in Madison Square Garden, New York City, where thirteen thousand McCarthyites roared approval of speeches supporting him and waved McCarthy-for-President signs. But it was too late.

On December 2 the Senate, by a vote of sixty-seven to twenty-two, publicly condemned McCarthy's tactics as "contemptuous, contumacious and denunciatory . . . highly improper . . . reprehensible . . . [marked by] a high degree of irresponsibility."

President Eisenhower administered the *coup de grace* by warmly congratulating the censure committee. No longer afraid of McCarthy's power, the nation's press applauded.

McCarthy's reign of terror was over. Little further attention was paid to his ranting; it was once more safe for Americans to believe in and trust the Bill of Rights. McCarthy died May 2, 1957, a Far Right extremist who had come closer than any other to becoming the first American *Fuhrer.*

Philippine United Nations spokesman Carlos P. Romulo, a good friend of the United States, said on June 19, 1955, "The Americans are so obfuscated by their hatred of Communism they can not think straight. Anti-Communism in the United States is a new form of national hysteria. The Americans' fear of Communism is shown by the ease with which they are swayed by demagogues who rise in popular favor by exploiting Communism as a national issue."

The criticism might also have been intended for Eisenhower's Secretary of State, John Foster Dulles, who was pursuing an extremist foreign policy. In 1954 he ordered the Central Intelligence Agency (CIA), headed by his brother Allen, to arm and direct right-wing Guatemalan exiles in an invasion of their country. This CIA coup overthrew the left-wing Arbenz Government, replacing it with a conservative regime.

Although the operation was kept secret in the United States, to avoid criticism, the origin of the *putsch* was no secret in Latin America. When Vice President Richard Nixon attempted a "good will tour" of South America, he was mobbed and assailed by hostile crowds. For a while, President Eisenhower thought he would have to send in the Marines to rescue Nixon.

The Dulles intensification of the Cold War won approval on the Far Right. A California lawyer on the National Strategy Committee of the American Security Council (ASC) declared, "I'm in favor of a preventive war. . . . If we have to blow up Moscow, that's too bad." The ASC, formed in 1955 by former FBI men, served as a private loyalty review board for 3,200 companies, investigating their employees for left-wing or "statist" (social welfare) sympathies.

In the ten years between 1955 and 1965, the Extreme Right expanded rapidly, despite the loss of McCarthy as a leader. According to Senator Frank Church of Idaho, its organizations proliferated at the rate of 22 percent a year. By 1963 its propaganda was being broadcast weekly over seven thousand radio stations. The Reverend Carl McIntire, who in 1958 had been heard over only one station, was now broadcasting daily on 617. His listeners were "informed" that the National Council of Churches, with forty million members, was riddled with Communists.

The Far Right picked up great strength among whites who were opposed to the black civil rights movement. Anti-black extremism was touched off on May 17, 1954, by a unanimous Supreme Court decision in the case of *Brown v. Board of Education* that ruled racial segregation in the public schools unconstitutional. The principle of "separate but equal" facilities was rejected, with schools ordered to desegregate.

To keep blacks from integrating schools, lunch counters, motels, theaters, and comfort stations, Mississippi extremists organized the White Citizens Council, a movement that quickly spread to other Southern states. Black activists were roughed up, flung into jail, brutalized, and sometimes murdered.

On September 25, 1957, when black students attempted to enter Central High School in Little Rock, Arkansas, Governor Orval Faubus ordered state troops to keep them out. President Eisenhower forced Faubus to back down, but a segregationist mob then blocked the teenagers. The President was compelled to send a thousand paratroopers into Little Rock in full battle gear, the first time since the Reconstruction era that federal troops had been used to enforce black civil rights.

Nine black children, flanked by soldiers with fixed bayonets, finally succeeded in registering. Token integration, at least, had come at last to the South. Infuriated, Senator Richard Russell of Georgia accused the President of "applying tactics that must have been copied from the manual issued to the officers of Hitler's storm troopers."

Eisenhower replied coldly, "I must say that I completely fail to comprehend your comparison of our troops to Hitler's storm troopers. In one case military power was used to further the ambitions and purposes of a ruthless dictator; in the other to preserve the institutions of free government."

The leading and fastest-growing organization of the radical Right was the John Birch Society, named after an American Army officer reported to have been captured, tortured, and killed by North Korean Communists. The Society was organized in Indianapolis, Indiana, in December 1958, by Joseph Welch, a retired candy manufacturer and ex-director of the National Association of Manufacturers. Membership lists were secret; estimates of the number of Birchites in the US ranged from eighty thousand to four hundred thousand.

The Birchers infiltrated Republican organizations to capture them; disrupted school boards; harassed city councils and librarians; took over PTA's; boycotted Eleanor Roosevelt postage stamps; and furtively pasted Communist labels on Polish hams in stores. Their greatest accomplishment was capturing the 1964

Republican Convention to nominate Barry Goldwater for the Presidency on a Far Right platform.

Welch was convinced that Red agents and sympathizers had "full operational control" of the government, churches, schools, courts, press, and the American Medical Association. In a book he wrote called *The Politician,* he charged Eisenhower with being "a dedicated, conscious agent of the Communist conspiracy." Other Americans he named as Red agents were Milton Eisenhower, John Foster Dulles and his brother Allen, and General Marshall. He held Franklin D. Roosevelt guilty "of plain unadulterated treason." Nelson Rockefeller was planning "to make the United States a part of a one-world Socialist government." He wanted Chief Supreme Court Justice Earl Warren impeached for his crime in "converting this republic into a democracy." The Birchites did not consider that the Founding Fathers intended the United States to be a democracy.

Welch insisted that Norway, Iceland, Finland, and Hawaii were under Communist control; DeGaulle, Nehru, Nasser and Haile Selassie were Reds; Soviet space feats were fake; Red China had no atomic weapons; and that the Soviet Union was "just pretending to be against Red China."

The author asked ex-President Eisenhower, "Do you consider that the Birch Society and the lunatic fringe of the radical Right are as serious a menace to American democracy as the Nazi movement was in the days of the German Republic?"

"By no means," Eisenhower replied. "The groups referred to are either over-emotional or stupid. This includes Birchers, Ku Klux Klan, ultra liberals who want to eliminate ambition and self-reliance, and all Communists."

Fanatical or stupid, the Birch Society could not be taken lightly. When Democratic Congressman Ralph Harding criticized the Society in a House speech, he was praised by Drury Brown, Republican editor of the Blackfoot, Idaho, *Nexus.*

Brown found his car tires slashed, sugar in the gas tank, and a red swastika painted on the door. A woman phoned: "Last time it was your car. Next time it will be your home!"

Birchite money, membership, and influence were evident in many Far Right organizations. In 1960 the Texans for America, led by cattleman J. Evetts Haley, forced changes in history textbooks used in the state's public schools. They demanded censorship of any favorable mention of income tax; social security; farm subsidies; the TVA; federal school aid; the United Nations; disarmament; integration; General Marshall; the Supreme Court; the New Deal; the Fair Deal; the New Frontier; and any description of the United States as a democracy.

They demanded favorable mention for General MacArthur; Chiang Kai-shek; Calvin Coolidge; "traditional" presentations of Christianity; "patriotic wars"; and Senator McCarthy. Haley denied that Texans for America was a Birch Society branch, but admitted, "We share many of the same goals . . . and members."

Birchite influence was evident when the House Un-American Activities Committee subpoenaed 116 California teachers, then called off its "disloyalty" hearing, leaving the teachers under a cloud of public doubt. "The right-winger," Judge J. E. Barr of California's Siskiyou County Superior Court told the California Teachers Association, "when he becomes crazed with fear, will invariably strike out at the intellectuals whom he cannot understand and whose nonconformity he must, in his terror, equate with treason. . . . As long as this Rightist hysteria continues you school people must stand up and be counted or you will be shoved into a position where you dare not discuss, or teach . . . any subject except possibly a timid opinion on who is going to win the World Series."

Commenting on the House Un-American Activities Committee, British historian Arnold Toynbee wrote in *Life:* "This word 'un-American'! . . . 'A Committee on Un-British Activities for the British Parliament' would be so laughable it could not be done. Or can you imagine a 'Committee against Un-French Activities'? This has become worse over the years. When I first knew America, her position was much more secure. Now she feels very insecure abroad, and this could mean less tolerance for opposition opinion at home."

Following the defeat of Barry Goldwater by Lyndon B. Johnson in the 1964 elections, Robert B. DePugh, leader of the Minutemen, wrote in a newsletter to his secret army of twenty-five thousand self-styled "patriots": "The hopes of millions of Americans that the Communist tide could be stopped with ballots instead of bullets have turned to dust." A St. Petersburg, Florida, chapter of the Birch Society passed out a Minutemen newsletter that said: "If you are EVER going to buy a gun, BUY IT NOW! . . . Form a secret Minutemen team."

Senator Stephen M. Young of Ohio reported being told by a veteran diplomat of a European embassy, "One thing has always puzzled me about you Americans. You have nightmares about Communist demons burrowing from within. Yet for years American Fascists have grown increasingly dangerous and nobody seems disturbed—least of all your Congressmen."

But the combined forces of the Far Right, united behind a States Rights Party, could muster only 110,000 votes against President Eisenhower's re-election in 1956. Even weaker was the combined eighty-four thousand vote of the Far Left candidates for the Socialist, Socialist Labor, and Socialist Worker Parties.

Running for President also were Far Out extremist candidates. Henry Krajewski, a tavern owner and former New Jersey pig farmer, ran on the Poor Man's ticket with a pig for his emblem and his slogan, "Who wants to eat a donkey or elephant?" He promised free beer and lower income taxes. Vegetarian Party candidate Simon Gould of New York promised to turn America into a meatless society that would abolish war.

In the 1960 campaign a new Far Out group, the American Beat Concensus, nominated Chicago bookseller William Lloyd Smith on a platform that promised to abolish the working class, give artists a ten-billion-dollar subsidy, make peace with everybody, and legalize everything. The Beats were the first of America's new "society dropouts," characterized by beards, indifference to bathtubs, rejection of middle-class American ideals, non-conformism, and total absorption in self-expression.

The civil rights movement of the sixties began with the Reverend Martin Luther King's non-violent program of civil disobedience against racial injustice. On February 1, 1960, blacks denied service at variety store lunch counters in Greensboro, North Carolina, staged "sit-in" demonstrations, refusing to vacate lunch stools until closing time. By June over fifteen hundred had been arrested in sit-in demonstrations all over the South. White sympathizers up North picketed chain stores with a Southern color bar.

"The sit-ins," said Harold Flemming, Director of the Southern Regional Council, "were the psychological turning point in race relations in the South." But many young black intellectuals, impatient at the slow pace of integration, organized the Student Nonviolent Co-ordinating Committee (SNCC). Moving into rural communities of the South in 1962 and 1963 to organize black voter registration drives and protest marches, many of them were shot, beaten, gassed, whipped, and jailed.

In 1964 three civil rights workers in the Mississippi Summer Project—Andrew Goodman and Michael Schwerner, both white, and local James E. Chaney, black—were murdered by Southern white extremists. This atrocity and other die-hard acts

The Observer
"You people lower the tone of the locality."

of violence against peaceful civil rights activists angered young black leaders into counter-extremism.

Stokely Carmichael and H. Rap Brown stirred black crowds with appeals to answer violence by violence, arguing that the only dissent white America respected was "black power." Soon the nation was rocked by black riots in the cities.

An important act of Establishment extremism took place in April 1961, as a result of the decision by the CIA, State Department, and Pentagon to overthrow the Cuban regime of pro-Communist Fidel Castro by financing an invasion of American-trained Cuban exiles. President Kennedy, newly-elected, was convinced to let them go ahead with the plan.

The result was the disastrous Bay of Pigs adventure which not only failed, but gave the United States a black eye in South America and throughout the world. Afterwards Kennedy said ruefully to Senator William Fulbright, who had opposed this act of extremism, "How could I have agreed to such a stupid mistake!"

Rapidly deteriorating United States-Union of Soviet Socialist Republics relations, leading to the Cuban missile crisis, created an hysterical controversy over air raid shelters. The extremists quickly manifested their brand of Americanism. Father L. C. McHugh advised any owner of a bomb shelter to drive off other Americans seeking refuge by "whatever means will effectively deter their assault." A California civil defense coordinator urged his constituents to arm themselves and their shelters against other Americans in flight from Los Angeles.

In 1963, the year President Kennedy was assassinated, a study by Group Research, Inc., showed that expenditures by the radical Right had jumped from five million dollars in 1958 to over fourteen million dollars. In contrast, the most influential group left of center—the Americans for Democratic Action—had a 1963 budget of only $75,000. The "First National Directory of 'Rightist' Groups, Publications and Some Individuals in the U.S.," published in 1962, listed 37 percent of the House of Representatives and 25 percent of the Senate.

On the West Coast, Dr. Fred C. Schwarz, heading a Far Right movement called the Christian Anti-Communism Crusade, was denounced at a Los Angeles rally on February 1, 1962. Speaking on "The Extreme Right—Threat to Democracy" were the Reverend John G. Simmons and the Reverend Brooks B. Walker. During the rally both ministers were informed that their homes had just been bombed. *Life* Magazine said, "Schwarz preaches doomsday by communism by 1973 unless every American starts distrusting his neighbor as a possible Communist or 'comsymp' [Communist sympathizer]." An enraged protest by powerful Schwarz backers who were *Life* advertisers brought publisher C. D. Jackson to a Schwarz rally in the Hollywood Bowl to apologize.

Another radical Right leader, Major General Edwin A. Walker, was relieved of his command in West Germany for propagandizing his troops with Birchite political doctrines. Resigning, he appeared before a Congressional committee to charge that he had been "muzzled." He accused Secretary of State Dean Rusk of being involved in a "control apparatus" of the government working in favor of Russia.

Time said, "It was a shoddy and confused display of name-calling without evidence." Even William F. Buckley Jr., a most articulate spokesman for the right, admitted, "The verdict is that General Walker be consigned to history's ashcan, and that henceforward his name call forth the roars of contempt and ridicule of a people." Walker was arrested at the University of Mississippi when he harangued a violent mob to prevent the registration of black student James Meredith.

A new sixties version of the old German American Bund, the American Nazi Party, recruited Fascist-minded extremists to the swastika banner of Hitler's admirer, George Lincoln Rockwell. Anti-semitic, anti-black the uniformed United States storm troopers were frequently arrested for starting street riots. They were defended by an organization they hated—the American Civil Liberties Union, which goes to court to uphold the liberties of all extremists under the Bill of Rights.

When Rockwell was shot to death by one of his own disgruntled followers, dying as he had lived, by violence, the funeral cortege bearing his body was denied entrance into a veterans' cemetery. Army authorities felt his burial there would be a desecration to thousands of American veterans in the cemetery who had died fighting the Nazis in Germany.

16

Extremism in the Sixties

No single act of extremism shocked Americans, and the world, more than the tragic event of November 22, 1963, when Lee Harvey Oswald assassinated John F. Kennedy as the President rode in a motorcade through downtown Dallas.

The Warren Commission investigation found no evidence that Oswald had been part of a conspiracy, but many critics disagreed. A flood of books and magazine articles presented new and re-analyzed evidence pointing to a right-wing plot. New Orleans District Attorney Jim Garrison indicted several individuals for involvement in such a conspiracy.

Kennedy's election had provoked a frenzy of hatred against him by Far Right Texans who loathed his liberalism, his Catholicism, and his support of civil rights. In the two years before his assassination, the Secret Service had to investigate thirty-four threats against his life from Texas.

Fortune magazine had noted that Joseph McCarthy's greatest support had come from Texas oil millionaires like Hugh Roy Cullen, who had declared, "I think Senator McCarthy is the greatest man in America." Texas billionaire H. L. Hunt financed a foundation to fight the income tax, Medicare, aid to education, mental health, the federal farm program, highway appropriations, urban renewal, foreign aid, and the United Nations.

The Far Right had been strongly active in Dallas just before Kennedy's visit. Four weeks earlier, during a visit to the city by America's United Nations delegate, Adlai Stevenson, extremists held an anti-United Nations demonstration addressed by General Walker. Dallas was flooded with handbills bearing the President's picture, full-face and profile like an FBI poster, and the message: "WANTED FOR TREASON. THIS MAN is wanted for treasonous activities against the United States."

When Stevenson tried to speak in a Dallas auditorium, he was hooted and driven out. A violent mob closed in on him, shouting obscenities and spitting at him. One woman hit him on the head with her sign. Stevenson asked in bewilderment, "Are these human beings or are these animals?"

The morning Kennedy came to Dallas, the Dallas *News* ran a full-page ad, paid for by the Extreme Right, inflaming hatred against him as a pro-Communist traitor. "How can people write such things?" the President exclaimed in disgust.

Hours later he was dead.

At the other end of the political spectrum, the Communist Party was no longer considered dynamic enough for radical leftists among college students and young blacks. Following Kennedy's election, a New Left began to take shape. Students for a Democratic Society (SDS) was organized in 1961, the mildest but most important of a dozen different left-of-center youth groups springing up in the sixties. SDS spearheaded anti-Vietnam demonstrations and anti-draft protests; they also co-operated with the black militants of SNCC.

On the extreme flank of the New Left was the Progressive Labor Party (PLP), openly espousing violence. When coal miners struck in Hazard, Kentucky, in 1963, the PLP sent several leaders there in a station wagon filled with guns and Marxist pamphlets. They were chased out of town by tough mining officials and the local police. In 1964 the PLP sought to intensify black rioting in Harlem. Oriented to Red China, the PLP damned the Soviet Union for "counter-revolutionary policies," and branded liberals and labor as "the true class enemy."

In May 1963, a shocking act of extremism in Birmingham, Alabama, turned millions of Americans against the Southern power structure. Local police, on orders from Public Safety Commissioner Eugene (Bull) Connor, were shown on TV as they swept peaceful black marchers off their feet with streams from high-pressure fire hoses, sent savage police dogs lunging at them, and beat them with clubs. One woman was seen pinioned to the sidewalk with a cop's knee on her throat. "Connor became an international symbol," *Time* noted, "of blind, cruel Southern racism." Also in Birmingham that year a black church was bombed, killing four children.

When a federal court ordered two black students admitted to the University of Alabama summer session, Governor George Wallace swore to bar them by "standing in the doorway." The Montgomery *Advertiser,* which formerly supported him, now concluded that he had "gone wild." President Kennedy federalized the Alabama National Guard and forced Wallace to back down.

Public sympathy was strongly with two hundred thousand Americans, black and white, who staged a giant march on Washington in August 1963, to demand "Freedom Now" for black Americans.

But the White Citizens Councils united in support of Governor Wallace, beginning the boom for his Presidential candidacy that flowered in 1968. Wallace represented the spirit of the "white backlash"—Americans in angry opposition to desegregation and the civil rights movement. Their extremism was manifested by bloody attacks on civil rights workers and marchers